The Great Divide

The
Great
Divide

Christianity OR Evolution

Gerard Berghoef
Lester DeKoster

The Christian's Library Press

ISBN: 0-934874-07-7

Copyright, 1988
Christian's Library Press, Inc.
P.O. Box 2226
Grand Rapids, Michigan 49501

Printed in the U.S.A.

For our children
and
grandchildren

"I have no greater joy than to hear that
my children walk in the truth."
III John, v. 4

"You turn things upside down!
Shall the potter be regarded as the clay;
that the thing made should say of its maker, 'He did not
make me';
or the thing formed say of him who formed it,
'He has no understanding'?"
(Isa. 29:16)

Has not God made foolish the wisdom of the world?
For the foolishness of God is wiser than men,
and the weakness of God is stronger than men.
(I Cor. 1:20, 25)

If you believed Moses, Jesus says, you would believe me,
for he wrote of me.
But if you do not believe his writings,
how will you believe my words?
(John 5:46–47)

Contents

PART ONE
The Plan of Redemption
Creation

Foreword

All religions are concerned with the reconciliation of man with God.

What is unique about Christianity is that God reaches out to man in His Plan of Redemption. In all other religions man reaches for God along routes of his own.

The uniqueness of Christianity is compromised by every effort to unite it with some form of evolution. Theistic evolution, also called "creationomic science," perverts Christianity into just another man-tailored religion. This is the thesis of this book.

We offer a report, a comparison and an invitation.

1. We report something of what may be seen to advantage for our own lives in the light of God's Word as revealed through Genesis.

2. We compare this "seeing" with the shadows cast

13

upon it by common secular evolution and theistic evolution, also in the version called "creationomic science."

3. We invite you to look along with us, and to discover some sightings on your own. There is much in Genesis awaiting the eye of faith; there is much in evolutionary theories awaiting exposure to the Light.

Secular evolutionists, on the whole, reject Genesis outright.

Theistic evolutionists reject Genesis by paying it lip-service. They label God's Word as primeval history, or poetry, or saga, myth or legend, to justify reading their own meanings into what Genesis says. The result is a hybrid "religion" mislabeled "Christianity" to mislead.

Our primary concern is to report, to compare and to invite you to join us in the process. As to persuasion, if God's Word does not persuade, whose word can? Our Lord Himself said, "And this is the judgment, that the light has come into the world, and men loved darkness rather than light . . . " (John 3:19).

To the Reader

Whenhen Israel was held in Egyptian slavery, it appeared that all the strength was Egypt's, all the weakness Israel's. It appeared that all of the science and wisdom were Egypt's, all of the ignorance Israel's.

But when God sent the ninth plague on Egypt, three days of thick darkness, Moses says of the Egyptians: "They saw not one another, neither rose any from his place for three days." All of the greatness and power of Egypt was immobilized at the divine command.

Of Israel, Moses writes: ". . . all the children of Israel had light in their dwellings" (Exod. 10:23).

We take this account as prophetic.

Where the Word of God is honored, there is light.

Where the words of man twist or oppose the Word of God, there is darkness.

So it is today when theories of evolution seem to have triumphed over divine revelation through Genesis. All the weight seems to be on the side of unbelief.

But, so is all the darkness! The light of the Word shines as brightly in Genesis today as it did for Israel in Egypt.

Convinced evolutionists, we know, are fully satisfied with their repudiation of Genesis. Theistic evolutionists subtly chop the Scriptures into straw for the bricks they build into temples of speculation. Both kinds of evolutionists claim the support of "scientific" evidence.

We will have something to say in Chapter 17 about the "SCIENCE" used by evolutionary theorizing. Upon examination, its support is not nearly so impressive, nor so unanimous, as the trusting are led to believe. Evolutionists do a lot of whistling in their darkness. And the darkness *is* with these modern Egyptians, while the Light still radiates from Genesis!

In a "Final Accounting" at the end we will draw the balance-sheet on:

1. God's Plan of Redemption which structures Christianity, and,

2. Its rejection by secular evolution, and,

3. Its perversion into a man-made religion by theistic evolution.

We use the term *theistic evolution* for all the various efforts to adapt the Bible, openly or deceptively, to theories of man's animal ancestry. A sampling of such hybrids appears in our Book Note, including an attempt under the label of "creationomic science."

The theistic evolutionist concedes the day to evolutionary theorizing, and shreds the Bible accordingly. We do not join him. Neither should you.

We think it is obvious that if the Bible is twisted to accommodate evolutionary theory, then the Word of God is subordinated to the words of man. The infallible Author-ity of God's Word has been lost to the fallible author-ity of man's words. Whether this is done openly, or by "explaining" God's Word away, the cost to believer, Church and society is the same. Christianity has been perverted into another religion.

Evolution is but another form of the countless attacks launched by unbelief upon the Bible across the centuries. They all look impressive at the time: scepticism, philosophy, Reason, "science" and now evolution. But the attackers die away, while the Bible remains: "Heaven and earth will pass away, but my words will not pass away" (Matt. 24:25). This *is* the Word of the Lord, a "Rock" upon which to build for time and forever.

For brevity, we will generally be using the blanket term *evolution* to refer to all evolutionary theories, both secular and theistic.

Some of the sources we have found helpful are listed in the Book Note.

The Plan of Redemption

Across the centuries the Church has proclaimed the Plan of Redemption, derived from the Scriptures.

The elements of the Plan are well known. We structure this book by them.

What happens to the Plan of Redemption when the theory of man's evolution out of an animal ancestry is forced on it?

The hybrid which results turns out to be just another man-made religion masquerading as Christianity – an obvious attempt to make God serve the interests of man huckstered as man's service of God.

We can sympathize with the weakness of those who are overwhelmed by the so-called "evidence" for evolution, mistaken as we think them to be. But we find no sympathy, nor understanding, for deceptive efforts to blend Christianity and evolution into theistic evolution, also called "creationomic science."

Christianity declines to be yoked with unbelief, even when unbelief volubly claims to take the Bible "seriously." For, as St. Paul puts it, "What fellowship has light with darkness?" (II Cor. 6:14).

Let us briefly preview here the darkness which theistic evolution seeks to impose on God's Plan of Redemption. Later chapters will extend and elaborate this summary.

Creation

1. *Light*: for Christianity, "in the beginning" God created all things through His Word, who became incarnate in Jesus Christ.

Darkness: for theistic evolution, God initiated the universe through a burst of energy called the "Big Bang." But this Bang was not a Word, and never became incarnate in Jesus Christ.

2. *Light*: for Christianity, God spoke all things into being in six distinct and separate creative events, divided into six days, followed by a day of rest.

Darkness: for theistic evolution, the evolutionary process begun with the Bang proceeds in uninterrupted sequence; indeed any interference by God, who is used only to sustain the creation in being, is forbidden.

3. *Light*: for Christianity, God made man as an adult, gifted with God's image and "very good."

Darkness: for theistic evolution, man slowly emerges from the animal, never was "very good" and bears no divine image.

Fall

4. *Light*: for Christianity, man deliberately chooses to violate God's Word of command, and this sin admits death to human history.

Darkness: theistic evolution knows nothing of a divine "probationary command," knows nothing of a "Fall"—what perfection could evolutionary man fall from?—and naturalizes death as simply the exhaustion of vital energies.

5. *Light*: for Christianity, the Fall leaves humanity incapable of restoring the communion with God which is "life." Man is depraved at birth.

Darkness: for theistic evolution, sin can hardly be defined, and human evil reflects where man is on the evolutionary totem pole.

Incarnation

6. *Light*: for Christianity, because the Fall and human depravity are man's responsibility, God can out of love, assume in Christ the penalty of death upon sin, thus opening a way for man's redemption through faith.

Darkness: for theistic evolution, because human imperfection only reflects the temporal lag in God's evolutionary "strategy," if Christ were sent to die on Calvary it could only be to compensate His Father's shortfall.

7. *Light*: for Christianity, the creating Word is incarnate in Jesus Christ to become "the Lamb of God who takes away the sin of the world," as foreshadowed in the Old Testament ceremonial law and the prophets.

Darkness: for theistic evolution, the Old Testa-

ment is variously mutilated to start with the Exodus, to
begin as myth or primal history, providing no basis in
God's dealing with man from the beginning which
would explain Israel's ceremonial law or Christ's vicarious death.

There is more, as will appear in the sequel.

But it is clear to all but the wilfully misled that the
Christianity which from the beginning has come into
history as out of, and built around, the Plan of Redemption cannot be whatever "religion" is forged out of some
forced union of Christianity and evolution.

"What has a believer in common with an unbe-
liever?" (II Cor. 6:15).

The Plan of Redemption
Creation

GENESIS

Reveals that in the beginning there was the God who further reveals Himself, as we confess in the Apostles Creed, as "God the Father Almighty."

EVOLUTION

Theorizes that in the beginning there was a burst of energy called the Big Bang.

THEISTIC EVOLUTION

Attempts to tie God and the Bang together, and in so doing begins its reduction of Christianity to the status of just another religion.

1

"In the Beginning . . ."

*G*enesis reports: "In the beginning, God . . ." (1:1).

Evolution theorizes: In the beginning . . . Bang!

Theistic evolution tries to join God and the Bang together. For these theorists, God blessed the Bang with His presence, and obligingly sustains the universe across billions of years so evolution can do His "strategy," and evolutionists their thing.

How are we to choose among them?

The answer to that crucial question is not to be found in arguing the "case" for or against evolution, nor in trying to prove the reliability of Genesis. Such arguments always bog down somewhere short of conviction.

The answer begins in learning to see how choice is

made, namely that all depends upon what we bring to
making the decision.

What do we bring to decision-making about Genesis?

1. For Christianity, the Bible supplies the answer:
"By *faith* we understand that the world was created by
the word of God, so that what is seen was made out of
things which do not appear" (Heb. 11:3).

2. Evolution, too, is accepted finally by an act of
belief. To distinguish such "faith" from that of the
Bible, we call it *credulity*.

3. Theistic evolution or "creationomic science" (we
will usually just use the first term to mean both) is also
held for true by an act of belief. Let us call it *gullibility*–you will see why as we proceed through this
book.

What these three options all have in common is this:
they come to us in words. And belief, or disbelief, is our
only mode of response to words.

1. **Faith** opens the believer to the power of the Word
of God, as revealed in the Scriptures, and enables that
Word to govern our thinking, our own words, and our
behavior.

2. **Credulity** opens us to the words of others, and
enables these words to govern our thinking, our own
words and our behavior.

3. **Gullibility** is credulity misplaced, and opens us to
control by the Lie of the Prince of Lies who then rules
our thinking, our own words and our behavior.

Words have their authors. They are spoken, or written, by someone.

This author becomes our author-ity for accepting his
word as true.

The Author-ity of the Scriptures is God.

The author-ity of men's words is one or another human being.

The author-ity for the Lie is the Devil.

Which, then, of the three options do we accept and commend to you: (1) "in the beginning, God;" or, (2) in the beginning, Bang; or (3) in the beginning some contrived union of the two?

For us it is, "In the beginning, God . . ." (Gen. 1:1).

This means that God is active in and through His creation from the beginning to this moment. "Our God is in the heavens," says the psalmist, "he does whatever he pleases" (Ps. 115:3). The breezes are His whispers, the birds His voice, the harvest His production, the sunshine and the rain His messengers. Not (as theistic evolution holds) because He once set the universe off on its lawful way, nor because He can be imagined as somehow participant in what can be traced as "natural law." No, the Bible reveals a God who uses His creation, here and now, for personal communion with all who believe, in accord with every one's need.

Theistic evolution pays lip service to the omnipresence of God. But its "God" is bound by the "principle of uniformity" which science needs to validate its calculations. God's activity is limited to insuring that the processes of nature go on without interruption. If God did communicate through the sunset, for example, it would only be in accord with the "laws" of physics and meteorology. God is so bound by "uniformity" that "today is the product of yesterday"–precisely opposite to the freedom Christianity holds out to faith, the hope Christianity holds out to prayer.

No, when "In the beginning, God" is adapted to "In the beginning, Bang," the result is naturalized religion, not Christianity.

Believers rejoice that at this moment God is free and willing to adapt all that He has made and sustains to the service of His will for the believer's life. He can "give his angels charge of you, to guard you in all your ways," whatever those ways may be. And they will "bear you up in their hands, lest you dash your foot against a stone" (Ps. 91:11–12). For Christianity, no "principle of uniformity" can come between us and the active love of God. No hair, indeed, can fall from our heads without His active will (Matt. 10:30).

The Great Divide *is* there.

It's either: God and Christianity **OR** evolution and the Bang.

2

GENESIS

Reveals that God used speech as His mode of bringing all things into existence. The vehicle of speech is the Word. St. John confirms the Genesis account of creation as he reveals that this creating Word was the Son of God who became incarnate as Jesus Christ.

EVOLUTION

Theorizes that all things develop out of the Bang, over billions of years, in an evolutionary sequence which is in fact riddled by man's inability to establish all the crucial "missing links."

THEISTIC EVOLUTION

Fancies that God can be bent to the service of evolutionary theory by conceding Him the right to act as origin of the Bang and preserver of whatever evolves, while restricting His participation to what man can confirm of His evolutionary "strategy" back to the Bang. In short, God serves the purposes of "science" without the right of any divine interference with the required "uniformity" of "natural law." Christ is not recognized as the creating Word, but gets added onto evolution as "Savior," a division which tries to separate the "Word" of St. John's Prologue from the Word who "became flesh" in Jesus Christ. What results is a caricature of Christianity.

2

"And God Said . . ."
(Gen. 1:3, etc.)

God spoke creation into existence. And God thus sets the "Word" at the center of divine revelation and of Christianity right from "the beginning."

But, God didn't say, "Bang!"

Not according to Genesis. *And why should a loving Father lie to His children about it?* The one who deals in gullibility is the Devil.

The God of Christianity is a person. God persistently reveals Himself through the Scriptures as person. Persons speak. Speech is a freely chosen act. God reveals His independence of natural law "uniformity," as we do ours, in speech.

Genesis clearly discriminates the God who was "in

the beginning" from the "God" of theistic evolution. In ways like these:

1. In Genesis, God speaks; in theistic evolution God presides over a burst of energy recently called the "Big Bang."

Quite different conceptions of God, don't you think?

2. The God of Genesis creates all things through His Word.

The God of theistic evolution sustains evolutionary processes which gradually bring things into existence.

Quite different conceptions of God, don't you think?

3. St. John reveals that the Word through whom God spoke the creation is the Son who "became flesh and dwelt among us" (John 1:14).

Theistic evolution pays lip service to Jesus the Christ, but robs Him of His role "in the beginning," and is deaf to St. John's confirmation of the Genesis creation account.

A totally different conception of the Christ, too, isn't it?

In fact, a totally different conception of Christianity!

Perhaps you are already coming to see why we speak of theistic evolution as only for the gullible.

Faith hears in each, "And God said. . ." of Genesis a prophecy of Christ; and observes in each rejection of, "And God said. . ." by evolutionary theory a rejection of Christ. For He is the Word "through whom all things were made" (John 1:3).

And what does this mean to you, here and now?

A great deal, if you wish to live Christianly in the world.

The creative priority of the Word, established in Genesis but rejected by evolution, becomes central to the Bible and thus to Christianity itself.

Let us only list, briefly, some of the strands flowing out of, "And God said . . ." in Genesis and incorporated into Christianity and the Christian life:

1. Speech becomes the mode of God's communication with man, that is with you. Like creation, so also revelation is the fruit of the Word.

2. Through God's revelation, the Genesis account is confirmed by the Word of the psalmists, like this: "By the word of the Lord the heavens were made, and all their host by the breath of his mouth . . . For he spoke, and it came to be; he commanded, and it stood fast" (Ps. 33:6, 9). And in the New Testament: "In many and various ways God spoke of old to our fathers by the prophets; but in these last days he has spoken to us by a Son, whom he appointed heir of all things, through whom also he created the world" (Heb. 1:1–2). The Bible is unrelenting witness to Word-creation, and thus weaves the Genesis revelation into Christianity.

3. The "Jesus" of theistic evolution is cut loose from His Genesis foundation, but this divorces Him from the Prologue to St. John's Gospel as well. For John reveals that: "In the beginning was the Word, and the Word was with God and the Word was God. He was in the beginning with God; all things were made through him, and without him was not anything made which was made" (John 1:1–3). Your salvation depends on the creating Word who became flesh and lived and died for us. St. John identifies Jesus the Savior with Jesus the Agent of God's creation as revealed in Genesis. Only this Jesus is the heart of Christianity.

4. Because the creation was done in visible syllables

of divine speech, the whole universe can "speak" God's glory to you: "The heavens are telling the glory of God; and the firmament proclaims his handiwork. Day unto day pours forth speech, and night unto night declares knowledge" (Ps. 19:1–2).

5. The Word of God is the Father's Agent in providential care and control of all that He has made: ". . . upholding the universe by the word of his power" (Heb. 1:3).

God "calls" the stars "by name," Isaiah says; "by the greatness of his might and because he is strong in power not one is missing." You can take the prophet's advice, then, to, "Lift up your eyes on high and see: who created these?" (Isa. 40:26). And you can catch the nuance of difference between Christianity and evolution. It is not "how did these evolve?" but "who created these?"

6. We are able to understand, when we remember that Christ is the creating Word, how He can still the waves of the Galilean sea *with a Word*: "Then he rose and rebuked the winds and the sea; and there was a great calm" (Matt. 8:26). Observe well this divine intrusion on the evolutionist's cherished principle of uniformity. His God is supposed to remain "external" to the universe. But that is not the God of Christianity, nor the Word who is the Christ.

But the same divine, free intrusion on the uniformity of "natural law" reappears (as is true of all the Lord's miracles) in Jesus' raising of Lazarus through speech; God re-creates as He creates: "Jesus cried with a loud voice, 'Lazarus, come out.' The dead man came out . . ." (John 11:43–44). The same Word who offers new life to us *through faith*!

7. And God uses the inspired Word of the Scriptures

to create in us the faith which receives His revelation as true: "So faith comes from what is heard..." (Rom. 10:17).

8. Proclamation of the Word is the primary task of the Church: "Go into all the world and preach the gospel..." (Mark 16:15) is the Lord's command to the apostles representing His Church. To which St. Paul adds, "And how are they to hear without a preacher? And how can men preach unless they are sent? As it is written, 'How beautiful are the feet of those who preach good news!'" (Rom. 10:14–15). We all receive the Gospel through the inspired Word.

The Bible does, indeed, use the term *Word* in a number of different ways. But the reference is always the same: the term *Word* represents God's chosen means of communion as fitted to the occasion. "Word" points the means of sharing as between God and His creation, God and His people, God and the world. Which form of the "Word" God is using becomes clear from the biblical context. And always, the appeal is to faith. Word and faith are correlatives.

The "Word" introduced in Genesis with, "And God said...," which is rejected by theistic evolution, is in fact woven into the Scriptures, into the heart of Christianity, into the life of the believer.

It is always:

Christianity **OR** evolution.

GENESIS

Reveals that on the first day of creation, God spoke light into existence.

EVOLUTION

and

THEISTIC EVOLUTION

Suppose that light is inconceivable without its physical vehicles, like sun, moon, and stars.

3

"Let There Be Light..."
(Gen. 1:3)

The Word of God sheds light.

This we are to learn first of all from the Scriptures.

Where must man go for "light" on how life is to be lived?

To the Word of God.

Where must we go for "light" on our origin and destiny?

To the Word of God.

So Genesis reports that God put light first: "And God said, 'Let there be light.' And there was light" (Gen. 1:3).

It has been the experience of the faithful ever since: God's Word illumines. It illumines in such a way that sunlight is but its symbol.

But the light of the Genesis Word is excluded from the world of the evolutionists.

Evolutionary theorists ransack their brains to grasp how Genesis can report the creation of "light" on the first day, while reporting the creation of light's vehicles—sun, moon, and stars—on the fourth day. Concluding that this is impossible, the evolutionists scoff a little (or more) at those who believe Genesis. Who could be so foolish, the evolutionist laughs (witnessing to his materialism), as to imagine light without some physical source? How naive can you get?

He testifies reliably to one thing: the only kind of light he can imagine is physical light. That is why he is self-blinded to the "light" of God's Word.

And the evolutionist, therefore, misses one thing: if the Genesis account were a myth designed to deceive, if it were but a "cunningly devised fable" (II Peter 1:16), the writer would never have reported "light" before sun, moon, and stars. That would give the hoax away. The Deceiver would have feared that no one would believe such a record. It is a sign of the truth, as revealed through Genesis, that the seemingly impossible is exactly the way it was "in the beginning": light before the sun! As acceptable to faith as incredible to gullibility.

God *did* speak light into existence, first of all, to instruct the faithful where to look for His light on their lives: to His Word.

There is one source of an infallible light on life, and duty, and destiny, and salvation, and judgment: the Word-Scriptures which are "a lamp to my feet, and a light to my path" (Ps. 119:105).

God's Word gives light. But this is not simply poetic or metaphorical language. Just as the rising sun illumines the world about us, so the Word of God illumines for us the circumstances under which we live, the choices we are obliged to make, the issues of life itself. Just as we can walk in sunlight without stumbling, so we tread the path of life in the light of the Word with sure step. Again, just as the rising of the sun shatters the darkness of night, so the shining of the light of the Word shatters the darkness of our ignorance, and liberates the believer from bondage to the Lie of the Devil. It is hardly surprising that such "light" is unknown among the shadowy speculations of evolutionism.

Like the thread of the Word, so the thread of "light" is woven everywhere into the texture of the Bible and Christianity.

Thus, St. Paul not only confirms the Genesis account but also immediately attaches it to Jesus: "For it is the God who said, 'Let light shine out of darkness,' who has shone in our hearts to give the light of the knowledge of the glory of God in the face of Christ" (II Cor. 4:6). What the evolutionist counts the folly of the Genesis account, St. Paul counts a testimony to Jesus the Christ.

The evolutionist who rejects Genesis, or explains it away, obviously prefers the darkness from which the believer is liberated: "The people who walked in darkness have seen a great light; those who dwelt in a land of deep darkness, on them has light shined" (Isa. 9:2). Yes, true, if the Word be received in faith.

Jesus makes the application: "Walk while you have the light, lest the darkness overtake you; he who walks in the darkness does not know where he goes. While you have the light, believe in the light, that you may become sons of light" (John 12:35). Truth open to faith; closed to gullibility.

The light created on the first day will outlast the sun,

of course, and is in no way dependent on it. Speaking of the New Jerusalem, St. John tells us: "And night shall be no more; they have no need of lamp or sun, for the Lord God will be their light . . ." (Rev. 22:5).

John echoes the words of Isaiah: "The sun shall be no more your light by day, nor for brightness shall the moon give light to you by night; but the Lord shall be your everlasting light, and your God will be your glory" (Isa. 60:19). It all begins with, "And God said, 'Let there be light' . . . ."

As a footnote, let us add that there is an interesting parallel to the light-giving power of God's Word in our own use of words, true because we ourselves are made in God's image.

Suppose some problem puzzles you. And then someone explains it to you, in words of course.

Suddenly you catch on, and what do you say?

Is it, "Thanks, now I *hear*"?

No, you say, "Thanks, now I *see*."

Odd?

Not at all. Because we are made in the image of the Word-using God, whose Word calls light into being, our words too can shed their own kind of light.

Moreover, as David suggests, when the faith-ful set the light of their words in the Light of God's Word, then there can be true advance in wisdom and understanding: "In thy light do we see [our] light" (Ps. 36:9).

But evolutionists decline to see their "light" in the illumination of God's Light. This is why they appeal to the credulous and the gullible, but not to faith.

It is either:

"And God said, 'Let there be light'; and there was light," **OR** darkness.

4

GENESIS

Reveals that God makes man in His own image.

EVOLUTION

and

THEISTIC EVOLUTION

Surmise that man has evolved from the animal—which of course has no image to pass along, at least none that man would care to inherit.

4

"Let Us Make Man in Our Image . . ."
(Gen. 1:26)

God chooses to start man from the top. So Genesis reveals.

Evolution chooses to start man from the bottom. So men surmise, thus rejecting or perverting the Genesis revelation.

Theistic evolution pretends to bridge this yawning chasm, but finds no way to harmonize man as image-bearer of God with man as heir of the animal.

Christianity OR evolution!

And what does creation in God's image mean to you? Much in every way.

1. To begin with, that is the true source of your own

self-image. Do you see yourself when the poet speaks of fallen man as "a wounded angel"? There is great hope in that poetic license when tempered in the light of the Word.

OR do you see yourself as what one writer calls "the trousered ape," the best that the animal can produce so far?

No hope in it. All those billions of years to get to this? With an animal yesterday and no real tomorrow?

2. You can have a high destiny, promised all who believe, through the same creating Word who will re-create the new heaven and new earth. This is the Genesis theme as developed throughout the Scriptures and into Christianity.

OR are you mired in the improbable hope that across aeons of time some man may altogether shrug off his animal ancestry? This is the extent of evolutionary hope, which theistic evolution tries to drape a little in trappings it selectively purloins from the Scriptures.

3. This is how the psalmist describes you as seen through the eye of faith and in the light of revelation: "When I look at thy heavens, the work of thy fingers, the moon and the stars which thou hast established; what is man that thou art mindful of him, and the son of man that thou dost care for him? Yet thou hast made him a little less than God, and dost crown him with glory and honor. Thou hast given him dominion over the works of thy hands; thou hast put all things under his feet, all sheep and oxen, and also the beasts of the field, the birds of the air, and the fish of the sea, and whatever passes along the paths of the sea" (Ps. 8:3–8).

This is but a variation on a Genesis theme: "Then God said, 'Let us make man in our image, after our likeness; and let them have dominion over the fish of the sea, and over the birds of the air, and over the cattle, and over all the earth'" (Gen. 1:26).

Christianity views us as God's image-bearers, an image marred indeed but not wholly lost in man's Fall.

4. Observe with the eye of faith how the gift of God's image is reflected in man's ability to create civilization, and to develop the vast mosaic of human culture. The animal has no such resources to give.

5. The image is key to invention, to vision, to the breathtaking achievements of true science and technology. The gift of the image provides the Holy Spirit with all the talents He deploys to make the "City" possible.

Compare this Christian view with the pitiful antecedents postulated by evolution of either variety.

1. If man be but some variety of the animal, how does one account for the rise and extent of human accomplishment? Does the beehive, the ant hill, the animal pack account for the glories of human creativity, the vast extent and organization of Metropolis? Surely only the gullible can believe that, those who want to "suppress the truth in unrighteousness" (Rom. 1:18).

2. Still more, what base, then, for the future?

Must you forlornly seek hope with some theistic evolutionists in fantasizing that man may one day, aeons hence, evolve into an immortal species? Some evolutionists so delude themselves, rather than yield to faith, thus fulfilling the apostle's prediction: "Therefore God sends upon them a strong delusion, to make them believe what is false, so that all may be condemned who did not believe the truth but had pleasure in unrighteousness" (II Thess. 2:11–12).

The Divide looms clear enough: man as heir of the image, to which all of man's achievements bear eloquent witness; or man as heir of the animal, a fantasy contradicted by civilization and culture themselves. What legitimate claim has animal ancestry on the marvels man has wrought?

We may learn something of the dimensions implicit in God's image by reflecting on what must have been God's anticipations for man as originally created—surely to be fulfilled in man's re-creation by the Word.

Say that "in the beginning" this Father made the universe as a kind of "playhouse" for His children, and gave them His image so that they could "subdue" the earth and, no doubt, lift their eyes to further conquests.

No true father, least of all God the Father Almighty, provides his children with a playhouse which they cannot use and enjoy.

What God had in view for man to subdue is suggested by the dimensions of the universe. The vastness, depth, and detail of the creation all point to the potential which God invested in man. What outskirts of the creation might even now be ours, what glories of culture and attainment, had man *not* fallen (see chapter 10). And what anticipation beckons redeemed image-bearers in the New Heaven and New Earth promised those who believe: "What no eye has seen, nor ear heard, nor the heart of man conceived, that God has prepared for those who love him" (I Cor. 2:9).

Yes, theistic evolution wants "in" on promises like these, while evolution rejects them as myth.

But like evolution itself, theistic evolution abandons the entire framework which Christianity erects, starting with Genesis, which alone founds such promises upon reality.

A Bible out of which the theistic evolutionist selects

just those passages which please him, while he lives in the disobedience of unbelief in regard to the rest, is a Word which he wishes to bend to his service. The Word is to serve him; not he the Word.

Theistic evolution makes an idol, according to its own image, by highly selective use of the Bible. It is repetition of an old blunder.

The idolater cuts a tree, Isaiah says, and "takes part of it and warms himself, he kindles a fire and bakes bread; also he makes a god and worships it, he makes it a graven image and falls down before it. Half of it he burns in the fire; over the half he eats flesh, he roasts meat and is satisfied; also he warms himself and says, 'Aha, I am warm, I have seen the fire.' And the rest of it he makes into a god, his idol; and falls down to it and worships it; he prays to it and says, 'Deliver me, for thou art my god'" (Isa. 44:15–17).

But what future was there, then, for such as these forerunners of theistic evolution?

"They know not, neither do they discern," the prophet says, "for he has shut their eyes, so they cannot see, and their minds, so that they cannot understand" (Isa. 44:18).

The Divide: are you made in the Image of God, *OR* in the image of the lower animal? Or did God somehow, somewhere intrude His image on the evolutionary process in which, remember, the principal of uniformity forbids Him to interfere? If you can believe that man is thus able to twist God into the service of his theories, while flouting the Word as revealed in the Scriptures, you are exactly what evolutionists are looking for, someone gullible enough to believe anything.

GENESIS

Reveals that God made man "a living soul" by breathing into his nostrils the breath (Spirit) of life.

EVOLUTION

and

THEISTIC EVOLUTION

Theorize that human life is no different in kind from that of the animals, from which man's life presumably came.

5

"And Man Became a Living Soul . . ."
(Gen. 2:7)

The Bible takes its own view of "life" and of its opposite "death."

Evolution and theistic evolution limit the concept of "life" to what man could inherit from the animals. This is totally at odds with what the Bible reveals about "life" – and about "death" (see chapter 11).

The Bible makes clear that man, once called by God into being, *is* in being forever, something evolution ignores. For each of us the crucial issue is not whether we will survive time into eternity, but only how and where. Obviously, the animal world has no such eternity of being to give. There *is* a Divide between Christianity and evolution.

For evolution, what becomes animal "life" inexplicably emerges from the "dust" of inanimate matter. One, C. Lloyd Morgan, called it "emergent evolution"—without explanation, of course.

But Genesis flatly rejects the notion that dust can give birth to life. Dust has no such capacity.

This is clear from Genesis where God reveals that the dust out of which man was made has no "life" to pass along.

It was the boast of "science" not so long ago to have disproved the possibility of "spontaneous generation," that is of life originated out of the non-living.

But it has become the claim of evolution that a universe which started out as simply a burst of energy at some time mysteriously produced "life."

But hear the Genesis report: "And the Lord God formed man out of dust from the ground. . . ."

But, did the dust, then, become a "living" human being?

No, the dust, even when shaped as man by God Himself, clearly had no "life" to endow. Life came to man only after God ". . . breathed into his nostrils the breath of life; and man became a living soul" (Gen. 2:7–8).

Three steps there. Take note of them:

1. God forms man out of the dust from the ground. No life yet.

2. God breathes into man's nostrils. God's breath is His Spirit.

3. Then, and then only, does man become "a living soul."

In sum: even when God Himself has formed man out of the dust, there is no life in him. Obviously, the dust generates no life. The gift of life waits upon God's breathing into man's nostrils "the breath of life."

The impotency of dust is confirmed when God describes physical death as "return" to the dust (Gen. 3:19)–to precisely that lifelessness out of which evolution supposes life came by spontaneous generation.

This means that when the Bible speaks of "life," and evolution speaks of "life" they are talking about two very different things.

Now cross the Divide into evolutionary theory.

Evolution imagines that life somehow arose naturally out of lifeless matter. Theistic evolution supposes that through the "Bang" God somehow endowed the dust with its own power to generate life.

The Divide:

Either

"Life" is a supernatural endowment by God upon an otherwise lifeless creature of the lifeless dust–this is biblical;

Or

The dust acquires the power to produce "life" through the evolutionary process–which is not biblical at all.

The Divide becomes the sharper when we consider what the Bible refers to as the human "soul." Genesis, we observe, reports that in consequence of God's breathing into his nostrils, man becomes "a living soul."

Evolution thinks of man as a living animal, so much so that some theorists are fond of drawing parallels between human behavior and that of animal species. But God "breathes" nothing, of course, into evolutionary man. How could He interfere with the "principle of uniformity"?

Mysteriously, God's gift of the soul energizes the life of the body.

Man is a "living soul" through communion with God. This is the "life" which man forfeits at the Fall (see chapter 10), the "life" man can find restored through faith in Jesus Christ, according to the Plan of Redemption.

Physical life ceases at physical death, and the body is laid aside. Reunited as body/soul man stands before God at the Last Judgment. The redeemed are joined with God for "life" eternal, while the damned are alienated from Him in the "second death" (Rev. 21:8).

Participation in that "life" of communion with God which becomes eternal at the Last Day is available to us through the faith which opens the self to control by God's Word.

Of all this, evolution chooses to be ignorant.

For evolution the human being is but another instance of living organisms, so similar that the life of animal species can evolve into the animal life of man.

The themes of "soul" and "life" are mysterious. But we note once again the Great Divide widening here between Christianity and evolution.

1. For Christianity, man is made "a living soul" in the act of creation; for evolution man inherits "life" from the animal.

2. For Christianity, man forfeits all claim to "life" in the act of our first parents' disobedience; for evolution there has been no such act of original disobedience.

3. For Christianity, man finds access to "life" re-

stored through faith in the Word first revealed as, "And God said...;" for evolution Jesus is at most the "Reconciler" also evolved, lest the principle of uniformity be violated, out of animal antecedents.

God inspires Moses to say:

"See, I have set before you this day life and good, death and evil. If you obey the commandments of the Lord your God, which I command you this day, by loving the Lord your God, by walking in his ways, and by keeping his commandments and his statutes and his ordinances, then you shall live...therefore choose life..." (Deut. 30:15–16, 19).

Yes, choose life!

Genesis

Reveals that God made Eve (the mother of all living) out of Adam's side, thus keeping human flesh and blood separate and distinct.

Evolution

and

Theistic Evolution

Theorize that human flesh and blood simply evolved from that of the animal, and have no conception of one woman as mother of all living.

6

"The Rib . . . He Made into a Woman . . . "
(Gen. 2:22)

Why should God reveal through Genesis His special creation of woman, Eve, as done in a way which invites snickers from the credulous and gullible?

Here is the report: "So the Lord God caused a deep sleep to fall upon the man, and while he slept took one of his ribs and closed up its place with flesh; and the rib which the Lord God had taken from the man he made into a woman and brought her to the man. Then the man said, 'This at last is bone of my bones and flesh of my flesh; she shall be called Woman, because she was taken out of Man'" (Gen. 2:21–23).

"The man called his wife's name Eve, because she was the mother of all living" (Gen. 3:20).

Now, why should God have created Eve that way and especially revealed it to us?

Not, we may be sure, by coincidence, still less to furnish amusement to unbelief.

We think that at least two reasons are obvious:

1. One divine intention, discussed in the next chapter, was clearly to found the institution of human marriage on this unique creation of woman out of man's flesh.

2. Another purpose comes to light in St. John: "And the Word became flesh and dwelt among us" (John 1:14), coupled with the letter to the Hebrews: ". . . a body thou hast prepared for me" (Heb. 10:5). By carefully keeping human flesh unique and distinct, God was pre-arranging a "tabernacle" for the Advent of His Son into human history. We discuss this in chapter 13.

"Not all flesh is alike," writes St. Paul, "there is one kind for men, another for animals, another for birds, and another for fish" (I Cor. 18:39). This divinely intended distinction culminates in the unique creation of Eve.

God reveals His making of human flesh as done in two steps:

1. Adam is made of the dust of the earth.
2. Eve is made of the flesh of Adam.

Therefore, St. Paul can say to the skeptical Athenians that God, "hath made of one blood all nations of men to dwell on all the face of the earth" (Acts 17:26). It is the one blood of Adam which also coursed through the veins of Eve, and courses through the veins of us all. Animal blood does not replenish hospital blood banks.

For those willing to understand, the creation of Eve

is one of the foundation stones in the Plan of Redemption. Man and woman are destined to become one flesh in marriage, a model of Christ's relation to the Church (as we shall see); and Christ is destined to become of one flesh with mankind in the Incarnation, a flesh carefully prepared for His arrival from the foundation of the world.

All this is alien to both evolution and theistic evolution, so alien that jokes about Adam's rib bemuse the gullible.

Evolutionary theories further separate themselves from Christianity by deliberately blurring the boundary between human and animal flesh which the Bible so carefully establishes. Indeed, the evolutionist has no choice. Human flesh, on evolutionary theory, emerges from who knows what welter of antecedents?

Adam calls his wife "Eve" because, he says, she is "the mother of all living" (Gen. 3:20).

For centuries the Christian Church has been known as "the mother of believers," based on St. Paul's description: "But the Jerusalem above is free, and she is our mother" (Gal. 4:26).

But what has this to do with the Genesis account of the creation of Eve?

Take note:

1. St. Paul speaks of Adam as, ". . . a type of him who was to come" (Rom. 5:14). He stresses the parallel: "Thus it is written, 'The first man Adam became a living being'; the last Adam became a life-giving spirit" (I Cor. 15:45).

2. This parallel is not, of course, coincidental; nothing in divine revelation is. As we will note below, Eve

as "mother of all living" points unmistakably to the corporate unity of mankind. This universal unity is accented in the Fall (see chapter 10), and constitutes a foundation stone in the Plan of Redemption. This corporate unity through the flesh is transcended by the spiritual unity of the faithful in the Church, "the mother of believers."

3. This parallel between Eve as mother of all living and the Church as mother of all believers was vividly confirmed for the early Church Fathers in the Genesis account of the making of Eve, and St. John's account of Christ's death on the Cross. The Church has long seen the detailed Genesis description of the taking of Eve out of the *side* of the sleeping First Adam as prophetic. For out of the *side* of the Second Adam, "asleep" on the Cross, God took the symbols of the New Eve, the Church: "But one of the soldiers pierced his side with a spear, and at once there came out blood and water" (John 19:34)–the sacramental symbols of the Church!

No, it is not coincidence at all, as perceived through faith, that Genesis so minutely describes the making of Eve. Her making prefigures the symbolic making of the Church out of the side of Him who entered the flesh which Adam and Eve bequeathed to all mankind. And St. John is so much concerned that we shall take note of the flow of the Church's sacramental symbols from the side of the Second Adam that he goes on to say: "He who saw it has born witness–his testimony is true, and he knows that he tells the truth–that you also may believe" (John 19:35).

But how shall those blinded by evolution and theistic evolution "believe" the confirmation of Genesis by a soldier's spear?

Some theistic evolutionists, consistent with their rejection of Genesis, think of the New Eve, not as the Church, but as the Virgin Mary. By such distortion they seek to avoid any parallel between the First and Second Adam, and the making of Eve as prophetic of the emergence of the Church.

As always, there rises the Great Divide between Christianity and evolution.

Briefly note three correlative biblical mysteries which root in the uniqueness of Eve's creation—one flesh, one blood:

1. There is, according to Genesis, a corporate unity of all mankind implied in God's carefully taking Eve from Adam's side. This unity confirms the universal inheritance of the depravity produced by the Fall. This unity is reflected in the sense of human solidarity which transcends all the distortion wrought by sin and evil in human relations. This unity underlies such success as society has in uniting to develop civilization and culture. The "human family" is not an abstraction. In the creation of Eve it was fore-ordained a reality.

For such a "family" unity, of course, evolution can provide no foundation. It is not surprising that in an era which has been taken over by evolutionary theorizing the sense of human solidarity is disintegrating and Western society displays agonizing signs of coming apart at the seams. What else is to be expected when evolution supplants Christianity?

2. Man's organic unity out of Adam and Eve portends the spiritually organic unity of all believers in the Church, which can therefore be called the "Body" of Christ (Eph. 1:23), symbolically taken from His side.

Again, this "Body" finds no analogy in, and gets no impetus from, evolutionary theory.

Both of these profoundly Christian conceptions of corporate unity take their departure from the Genesis account of the creation of Adam and Eve.

3. And note only in summary fashion that out of the Genesis account of the making of Eve come these elements in the Plan of Redemption: (a) God made man one, unique flesh; (b) it is as one flesh that all mankind fell with Adam and Eve; (c) and, as will be discussed in chapter 13, it is that one flesh which the Son of Man assumed.

You can, of course, surrender all of the Light so graciously available to us through the inspired Word, in order to cling in the darkness to the alleged "scientific" certainties of evolutionary propaganda.

But at least be aware that in so doing you cross the Great Divide which separates Christianity from evolution.

On the one hand:

1. That unique flesh, first made Adam and then Eve, out of which all mankind corporately come, and into which, as we shall further point out, Jesus Christ descended through the Virgin Mary; the flesh which He carried back to heaven as token that all who believe are corporately united with Him, both now and forever,

OR

On the other hand:

2. Random flesh, evolved who knows whence and how, neither unifying man in corporate guilt and responsibility, nor into corporate societal life, nor able out of its resources to promise corporate unity with Christ in forgiveness and life eternal.

7

GENESIS

Reveals that through making Eve out of Adam's side God established forever the sanctity of human marriage, later revealed as model of the relation Christ sustains to His Bride, the Church.

EVOLUTION

and

THEISTIC EVOLUTION

Undermine the sanctity of marriage and stability of the home by bringing to it only the model of animal copulation and convenience.

7

"...And They Became One Flesh..."
(Gen. 2:24)

O n the basis of Genesis, Christianity affirms and sanctifies marriage and the family, the foundation of human society.

Evolution knows no marital sanctity, and brings only a heritage of animal copulation, encounters of convenience, abortion on demand. Theistic evolution may claim New Testament tributes to marriage and the family but cannot establish them, as Jesus Himself does, on Genesis.

If, on practical grounds, the case against evolutionary theory were based only on the devastation it has wrought in the family, it would be enough to condemn the fantasy of man's animal ancestry.

71

Jesus confirms the Genesis account of the sanctity of marriage and origin of the family in the very words of Genesis itself.

Asked about the legality of divorce, the Lord replies: "Have you not read that he who made them from the beginning, made them male and female, and said, 'For this reason a man shall leave his father and mother and be joined with his wife, and the two shall become one'? So they are no longer two but one. What therefore God has joined together, let no man put asunder" (Matt. 19:4–6, referring to Gen. 1:27 and quoting Gen. 2:24).

Take note:

1. Jesus here certifies as accurate the very language of Genesis, thus setting His authority against that of both evolution and theistic evolution in their rejection or distortion of Genesis.

2. Jesus confirms that God *made* man "in the beginning," and thus rejects theories of man's evolutionary development.

3. Jesus further confirms man's creation as adult male and female, ready for marriage. This both evolution and theistic evolution deny.

4. Jesus thus aligns Himself against all theories of man's evolutionary development. How can the theistic evolutionist, who rejects Jesus' certification of Genesis, still lay claim to being Jesus' disciple?

5. Jesus condemns precisely the casual laxity and the promiscuous sex, born of evolutionary theories. The "live-in" models animal behavior, but it caricatures marriage as theistic evolution caricatures Christianity. What barriers at all comparable to Christianity's commandments could evolution set against adultery?

Whose Word, then, will you heed: the Lord's OR the evolutionist's?

God counts the institution of marriage which He established "in the beginning" of such importance that He surrounds it with three of the Ten Commandments:

1. The Fifth: "Honor your father and your mother, that your days may be long in the land which the Lord your God gives you."

2. The Seventh: "You shall not commit adultery."

3. The Tenth: "You shall not covet...your neighbor's wife" (Exod. 20:12, 14, 17).

The evolutionist may hear these divine commands, and the theistic evolutionist may even endorse the New Testament affirmation of them, but his evolutionary theory undermines them all.

It *is* Christianity OR evolution!

And for you?

We are beneficiaries of the absolute societal centrality of marriage and the family, sustained by Christianity over the centuries as certified by divine revelation through Genesis.

There was a time when God's warning rang out from every marriage ceremony: "What God has joined together let no man put asunder."

Theories of evolution have deprived this solemn reminder of both its Author-ity and its voice.

The indissolubility of marriage and sanctity of the family are casualties on the road of evolutionary "progress." Only the evolutionist's denigration of the Bible is a greater crime against the stability of Western civilization.

St. Paul confirms the Genesis marriage theme and draws on it to warn against the indiscriminate sexual encounter so characteristic of the animal world: "Do you not know that he who joins himself to a prostitute becomes one body with her? For, as it is written, 'The two shall become one.' But he who is united with the Lord becomes one spirit with him. Shun immorality. Every other sin which a man commits is outside the body; but the immoral man sins against his own body" (I Cor. 6:16–18).

Christianity OR evolution!

Let us take note, in passing, that the Genesis-ordained centrality of the family in human society, and the Commandments-ordained centrality of the woman in the home confer upon motherhood a dignity and importance which no "liberation" movements can endow—but which evolutionary theorizing does much to undermine and destroy.

It is both man and woman who are the losers as evolution erodes the stability of the family.

Note finally, and note well, that the Genesis institution of the family is prophetic of Christ's own relationship to His Church.

Consider: after urging wives to be "subject in everything to their husbands," and "husbands to love their wives as their own bodies," St. Paul confirms these commands by quoting the Genesis account: "For this reason a man shall leave his father and mother and be joined to his wife, and the two shall become one" (Eph. 5:24, 28, 31).

Observe:

1. Here is further New Testament confirmation, if any were yet required, that the inspiring Spirit takes Genesis literally.

2. Here is further New Testament confirmation, too, if any more were yet required, that in rejecting Genesis

(as evolution does), or explaining its Word away (as theistic evolution does), the evolutionist sets himself against the very Spirit of Christianity.

But there is more.

Paul goes on from the Genesis quotation, that "the two shall become one," and writes: "This is a great mystery, and I take it to mean Christ and the church . . ." (Eph. 5:32).

Not only is the unique sanctity of marriage established by divine revelation in Genesis, but the mysterious relation of Christ to His Church is foretold there.

Theistic evolution volubly claims allegiance to the Church and her Lord, while rejecting or perverting the prefiguration of that holy union as revealed through Genesis. Only the gullible can think that possible.

St. Paul warns that those who refuse "to love the truth" become the victims of "strong delusion, to make them believe what is false" (II Thess. 2:10, 11).

What greater delusion might one suffer than not to see the chasm between:

1. Christianity which sanctifies marriage as instituted by God "in the beginning," designed to be foundation of human society and model for the relation between Christ and His Church, on the one hand, and

2. Evolution and theistic evolution find their model for marriage in passing animal encounter—a model which undermines marriage, is destroying the family, and thus sadly weakens the basic form of social stability.

GENESIS

Reveals that God created all things in the beginning, man included, as "very good."

EVOLUTION

and

THEISTIC EVOLUTION

Are confined to theorizing that man may in some era, millions of years hence, evolve into something like being "very good," a status far removed from the present evolutionary cycle.

8

"And Behold,
It Was Very Good..."
(Gen. 1:31)

All the mighty works of creation are done. They are done so well that God can "rest" in their perfection, as Genesis will next report.

"And God saw everything that he had made, and behold, it was very good. And there was evening and there was morning, a sixth day" (Gen. 1:31).

This inspired report sets a Divide between Christianity and all evolutionary theories of the origin of man. The evolutionists know nothing of a time when man could even be called "good," let alone "very good." The "god" whom theistic evolution tacks onto evolution cannot be the God of Christianity who made His creation "very good" in the beginning. The "word" which theistic evolution professes to honor as Jesus Christ cannot be the Word of God through whom all things were made "very good" at the beginning.

In short, it becomes increasingly evident that theistic evolution forges a religion of its own under the guise of "Christianity."

How are you involved by this Genesis status report?

God's creation of our first parents as "very good" clears God of all responsibility for man's not being "very good" as we know him now. Man's original perfection is God's work; man's historical imperfection is his own.

Here the Great Divide between Christianity and theistic evolution becomes absolute. Observe carefully:

1. Christianity teaches that God's condemnation of sin and evil, everywhere reported in the Bible, is His judgment on *man's* misbehavior, not on His own.

2. But for theistic evolution, God is Evolutionist-in-Charge of man's development from the Bang to the present. Man is the product of God's work. Whatever God finds wanting in man is of His own doing. How could God, then, condemn human misbehavior? Man is what God's evolutionary "strategy" has so far made us. Why all the fuming and threatening in the Bible over sin and evil? God is denouncing His own handiwork— on theistic evolutionary ground.

3. Still more, God's sincere desire for our redemption through faith in Jesus Christ comes into question. The promise of redemption made to Adam and Eve (see chapter 16) was not God's desire to overcome some evolutionary lag (for which He would be responsible, a

la theistic evolution), but His gracious offer to restore us to pre-Fall perfection.

4. And Jesus Christ is not sent to complete His theistic-evolutionary Father's half-done job. The Scripture nowhere even hints that Jesus takes on human flesh to correct the shortfall in His Father's evolutionary "strategy" as "creationomic science" calls it. Jesus comes, as the New Testament unmistakably teaches (See chapter 16) to bear the divine penalty on man's Fall from his original perfection.

Genesis reports man's Fall only after reporting man's perfect creation. Of course! Isn't a "Fall" meaningless unless man was first provided a height to fall from?

And let us bear in mind that our own personal hope for "restoration" in the Word of God, Jesus Christ, is meaningless except that man once had, through the same Word, an original perfection to which we can be restored.

This is obviously why, as we will observe (chapter 16), Jesus explains His mission to the world by starting with Genesis.

It is, then, at this point in the Genesis account, the report of man's creation as "very good," that theistic evolution can no longer obscure its departure from Christianity. Let us sum up what we have been saying:

Theistic evolution holds, in one form or another, that God has somehow supervised the evolution of man from the original burst of energy through primeval and animal stages to what man now is. God provides the setting; evolution is the process. God is Evolutionist-in-Charge; evolution is His technique.

The lie thus seems to provide the gullible with the advantage of having a foot in both worlds, in the safety of the Bible and the "with it" of evolutionary "science." They can be of the "in" crowd, and pious, too; "Christian" on Sunday, so to speak, and "scientific" the rest of the week. It's like standing with one foot in a row boat and with the other on the dock. It's a position that won't hold up.

Whatever "god" is imagined as in charge of the evolutionary process, He certainly is not the God of the Bible.

Consider:

1. If we had in Adam no original perfection, then Adam had no height to "fall" from, taking us down with him. That's theistic evolution. Is that good?

2. No, that's bad. For if we suffered no "Fall" from perfection in Adam, we have no lost perfection for Christ to restore.

3. Still worse, if God was involved in our being what we are now, who would redeem us? He's botched the job already.

4. Thus, the Christ in whom we hope for restoration has to be the Christ through whom all things were made "very good" in the beginning.

This is the Christ of Genesis. No other Christ can be genuine. No other "Christianity" can be, either.

9

GENESIS

Reveals that God's creating was done in separate steps on six separate days.

EVOLUTION

and

THEISTIC EVOLUTION

Theorize that living things evolved from non-living matter, and man evolved from the animals, in an uninterrupted process.

9

"And the Evening and the Morning Were the...Day"
(Gen. 1:5, etc.)

God is quite able and willing to liberate us from bondage to theories of evolution.

In fact, God obviously designed Genesis to offer that service. Genesis is inspired to leave theories of evolution grunting in the darkness.

How?

By reporting the creation in terms of seven discrete and separate "days." It's either this seven-day cycle OR evolution. It cannot be both.

Evolutionists stumble over the Genesis seven-day calendar, even though the calendars we all use bear weekly witness to the original.

So evolutionists claim that the daily creation cycle is meaningless; it is said to imply a nameless magician pulling tricks out of a hat; it is called myth or primal history; or it is held to imply long periods of time which the evolutionist will fill with his own fancies. In short, Genesis is said to mean anything but what Genesis plainly says.

Of course, evolution cannot rest easily with the divine revelation of a six-day creation and seventh-day rest cycle.

Why not?

Because a creation in discrete and separate acts flatly contradicts the evolutionary theory of long continuous development from one species into another. Genesis neatly checkmates Darwin long before he was born. And Darwin designs his hypothesis of continuous evolution in an effort to discredit Genesis.

The very term *evolution* means, briefly, that one form, or species, of existence evolves into another, and has done so all the way back to the Big Noise. To provide its theorizing with some claim to "science," evolution has to assume a stream of development without interruption from the Big Bang into the present. Still more, evolutionary "science" must also assume that this development proceeded in so orderly a fashion that a "principle of uniformity" governed every step.

What is that "principle"?

It is the assumption that the "laws" observed today are precisely the "laws" prevailing all the way back to the Big Bang. Else, of course, no reliable calculation of the past is possible. If the pace of development is not uniform, then there could be no "science," and no claim of "scientific" validity for Darwinian fictions.

Evolution admits no interruptions! No discrete and separate steps, lest the pattern be warped, computers rebel, and the gas let out of theories.

But the Genesis account is in fact full of interruptions. Six days worth of them! "Evening and morning" keep butting in all the time. God wanted it that way. Yes, we think with evolution clearly in view!

Genesis further annoys theistic evolutionary theorists by having God step into the creative process on each separate day, instead of His staying decently "outside" His universe so evolution can go smoothly along.

So Genesis is just a burr under the saddle of the evolutionist's hobby horse. No flow at all. No development from Day One into Day Two, and from Day Two into Day Three, etc. Exactly the opposite. All very separate, discrete acts of creation. In short, a plain rejection, right there "in the beginning," of evolutionary theorizing.

But why this revealed stress on *separate* days of creation? Couldn't God have spoken it all at once? Or couldn't He have called His "days" something like "aeons" or "ages," giving evolution room to theorize in? Those terms were available to the inspiring Spirit if that is what God meant to say through Genesis. Indeed, did God even need a day to create what Genesis reports for each separate occasion? Did He need longer to speak the Word than we take to read it?

No, we think the divine design and intent are evident. Genesis is written to show evolution the door! Which is why evolutionists of all sorts are so intent upon getting Genesis out of their way.

Genesis caps its creation account with what are also

persistent reminders of how far Christianity and evolution are apart, like these:

1. There is the matter of our Sunday, celebrating what was, for Genesis, the Sabbath Day: "Thus, the heavens and the earth were finished, all the host of them. And on the seventh day God finished his work which he had done, and he rested on the seventh day from all his work which he had done" (Gen. 2:2). Every seventh day of every week is a reminder to faith that God's creation and man's evolutionary theories cannot be merged together.

2. Evolution cannot have some "force" which "rests" on the evolutionary treadmill. And what achievement would it rest from? For evolution the developmental process grinds uniformly along. What could be the meaning of a "rest" and how would it fit into the computers which calculate those billions of years of continual development?

3. Theistic evolution has no room for a "resting" God either. This brand of evolutionary fantasizing also requires an uninterrupted development, on the principle of uniformity, one which has achieved no perfection to celebrate, no completed development to rest from. So the God of theistic evolution could not be the God who instituted the Sabbath. He could not be the God of Genesis at all.

So, then:

1. Every weekday reminds us that creation proceeded in strictly discrete and separate steps, precisely contrary to evolutionary theory.

2. Every Sunday reminds us that God clearly wants that contradiction to be unmistakable.

Genesis builds a Great Divide between Christianity and evolution, and obviously does it on purpose.

Those "Days"

Of course, the evolutionist will want to play games with the term *day*.

If you believe Genesis, you will be challenged to say what "day" means there.

And you will be treated to all sorts of guesses by "scholars" and "experts" made to show that the one thing Genesis cannot mean when it uses the term *day* is. . .just a day. Theologians and "experts" in Semitic languages will join the crowd. Even St. Augustine might be pressed into the service of understanding "day" as an aeon of time.

Thus will Genesis be twisted into seeming to mean what in fact it does not say. The term *is* "day." God the Holy Spirit inspired it.

And so, with all respect to Augustine and such abuse as is made of him, we think it's a sound rule to let the Bible—rather than the "expert"—be its own interpreter. The Reformation called this principle Sola Scriptura, solely the Bible.

What, on this principle, does God mean by "day" in Genesis?

We turn to another use of that term in the Bible.

How does Moses use it in reporting the fourth commandment, for example: "Remember the sabbath day to keep it holy. Six days you shall labor and do all your work. . . ."

The working day is familiar to us all. Even the evolutionist and the "expert" know what a day's work is, and claim their pay checks accordingly.

But, is our regular working day also the Genesis "day"?

Yes, God goes on to inspire Moses to say so: ". . . for in six days the Lord made heaven and earth, the sea and all that in them is, and rested the seventh day; therefore the Lord blessed the sabbath day and hallowed it" (Exod. 20:8–9, 11).

When all the "learned" clamor subsides, and all the guessing is heard no more, there the Word will stand: obviously, the "day" in "six days you shall labor . . ." and the "day" in "for in six days the Lord made . . ." mean the same period of time. Don't you think? Have you any ground for accusing God of the double talk characteristic of theistic evolutionists?

The Genesis week is our week. The Genesis day is our day. You would only look as foolish as the "expert" if you said, "Six indefinite periods of time – maybe several billion years each – you shall labor and do all your work. . . ." The "expert" and the evolutionist wouldn't really care to put in such working "days" for a pay check either. Who could blame them?

It is always better to let the Bible interpret itself than to let the "expert" misinterpret it for us.

Yes, Genesis was written to confute evolutionary theory. Not visible to gullibility, perhaps; but very clear to faith.

The Great Divide deepens as we go along.

Genesis means it that way.

PART TWO

The Plan of Redemption
The Fall

GENESIS

Reveals that man, made very good, chose to exercise the freedom included in the gift of God's image to disobey the divine command in what is known as "the Fall."

EVOLUTION

and

THEISTIC EVOLUTION

Lack all conception of a Fall, because they have no provision for man's ever being "very good."

10

"You Shall Not Eat..."
(Gen. 3:3)

John the Baptist, the forerunner of Jesus, introduces the Lord to the world as, "Behold the Lamb of God, who takes away the sin of the world" (John 1:29).

This description is clearly drawn from Israel's ceremonial law which required sacrifice for the forgiveness of sins.

The origin of this awesome ceremony lies in the Genesis account of man's Fall.

John the Baptist, like the apostle John, attaches Jesus to Genesis through the Old Testament history of Israel.

Take away Genesis, and Israel's ceremonial system has no anchor in history, and Christ's sacrificial death must be given another meaning—as it is in theistic evolutionary theory, where Christianity is perverted into another religion.

Man was made, as we have just observed, "very good."
Not according to evolutionary theory, but according to Christianity.

But man as we know ourselves and others is far from being "very good."
Something must have happened between the first creation and the rest of human history. How could the man made "very good" become man guilty of an endless variety of sins and evil? Where did the goodness go?
Only Genesis can tell us. Those deaf to Genesis through credulity or gullibility cannot hear the explanation. And at this point evolutionary theories decisively veer away from Christianity. It is a Great Divide that can be "healed" in words, but not in reality. For, the Genesis account of man's Fall is the occasion for instituting God's Plan of Redemption, the Plan which structures Christianity.

What is called the "problem of evil" has haunted the credulous and the gullible across the centuries. Philosophers, theologians, poets, and thinkers of all kinds have wrestled with their question of how a good God could have made or can endure a world full of sin and evil. Neither evolution nor theistic evolution can supply an answer. Those who reject Genesis, or explain it away, have no answer.

Yes, in Adam we all were made "very good."
We have God's Word on it.
But we are surrounded by a mire of sin and evil.

We have our own experience of it, though we will
need Genesis to help us understand just what "sin"
really is (chapter 12).

We are not told why the "mystery of iniquity"
(II Thess. 2:7) invaded God's good creation. But Genesis
does reveal how it happened.

By rejecting Genesis, or explaining it away, evolution detaches Christianity's Plan of Redemption from
its point of departure in man's Fall. What remains in
theistic evolution is a counterfeit gospel.

What did happen in the beginning, after man was
made "very good"?

The "very good" included the gift of God's image.

In the gift of God's image, lay the risk of man's
disobedience to God's will.

Why?

God is free. Man made in God's image is thus also
free.

But what, then, if man used his freedom to disobey
his Maker?

That was the risk of a "Fall" which, obviously, God
wanted to take, and we may surmise why.

God asked, and still asks, man's love.

But what, according to the Bible, is "love"?

"Love" implies freely given obedience. As Jesus puts
it: "If you love me, you will keep my commandments"
(John 14:15).

Notice, **IF** we *love* Him, we **WILL** keep the Lord's
commandments. That was the sign of love in the beginning; it is the sign of love for believers now.

Man found his "life" from the beginning, as we do
now, in communion with the living God, a communion
maintained through "love."

All of God's commandments to our first parents became, then, simple tests of their "love" for Him: obey
and live, that is, obey and enjoy communion with the
living God; disobey and die, for the communion is shattered. That is why the consequence of disobedience is
automatic: "You shall surely die."

That was not a vindictive display of anger. It was a
statement of fact. To "love," meaning to obey, is to keep
communion with God, which is "life."

To disobey, which is not to "love," is to break communion with God, which is "death."

One of God's rules given our first parents has been
called the "probationary command."

The command was this: "You may freely eat of every
tree of the garden; but of the tree of knowledge of good
and evil you shall not eat, for in the day that you eat of
it you shall surely die" (Gen. 2:16–17).

God can, and does, hold man responsible for his
behavior because man was made "very good," which
included freedom.

God asked freely-given obedience only of a man God
first made "very good," that is, gifted with His image to
be truly free. Of such a man, evolution has nothing to
say. It knows of none, and thus divides from Christianity and the Plan of Redemption.

We may say that God took at least a triple risk in
giving man the perfection of His image:

1. God's risk of losing the obedient love of man.

2. Man's risk of losing the communion with God
which the Bible calls "life."

3. God's risk of having to exercise His commitment

made "before the foundation of the world" (Eph. 1:4) to re-open for man the communion which is "life." God keeps that commitment by sending His only Son, Jesus Christ, as sacrificial "Lamb" to die for man's sin and evil.

Of this Jesus it is sung in heaven: "Worthy art thou to take the scroll and to open its seals, for thou wast slain and by thy blood did ransom men for God from every tribe and tongue and nation, and has made them a kingdom of priests to our God, and they shall reign on earth" (Rev. 5:9–10).

On this Christ rests our only hope of salvation. But this "Lamb of God" forms the heart of the Plan of Redemption only in the light of Genesis.

This is simple Christian doctrine, based on divine revelation and in one form or another reflected in all the creeds and catechisms of the Church, where theistic evolution finds no endorsement.

Transpose the Genesis account of the Fall into your own experience.

Like God, in whose image we are made, parents seek the freely given "love" of their children, and discover it reflected in willing obedience.

Even if a parent could program the child to absolute obedience, such obedience would obviously not be "love." It would be hollow and unsatisfying. Love must be freely given, or it is not love.

Thus the Genesis revelation commends itself to faith by coming in terms we can well understand.

We perceive how man made in God-given perfection could have used his freedom for the obedience of "love" which God desires. And we can perceive that man could also disobey, though we cannot explain why.

The "problem of evil" does not arise out of the tension between a good God and an evil world. Genesis has explained that. The "problem of evil" inheres in how a man made "very good" could choose sin over love. This Genesis does not explain.

The fruit of "the tree of the knowledge of good and evil" is forbidden. It becomes the test for freely given "love."

Our first parents ate of the forbidden fruit. This act of deliberate disobedience constituted the Fall with somber echoes across all of human history.

Adam and Eve were tempted by the "Father of Lies" (John 8:44) who speaks through a serpent. The serpent phrases what has become the standard form of temptation: "Did God say?" (Gen. 3:1).

Taken in, as are many nowadays, Eve replies that indeed God did say, "No!" But she has gone far enough to give the Devil an opening. The serpent suavely picks up the temptation; it is God, not he, who is the liar: "You will not die . . . you will be like God, knowing good and evil" (Gen. 3:1, 4).

So the woman "took of the fruit and ate; and she also gave some to her husband, and he ate" (Gen. 3:6).

The act of disobedience was done. The spiritual communion with God which is man's "life" was shattered. The physical death which symbolizes the spiritual alienation became inevitable. Death witnesses to the Fall throughout human history.

Man fell into "bondage to decay" (Rom. 8:21).

Genesis does not reveal why man sinned, nor how man even could sin. But the Genesis account is the only one we will receive of the intrusion of sin and evil on a world which God made "very good."

But, a talking serpent?

How naive can anyone be? Maybe in the Dark Ages, but not now!

Yes, the gullible scoff at the Genesis report of the temptation by way of a serpent, a talking serpent at that.

The scoffing is a measure of how great is the divide which separates biblical Christianity from its counterfeit in theistic evolution. For the account of the tempting serpent is woven into the Scriptures (Num. 21:6–9; Deut. 8:15; John 3:14–15; Rev. 12:9, 20:2, for example). Still more, this gullibility is exactly what St. Paul is expressly inspired to warn against: "But I am afraid that as the serpent deceived Eve by his cunning, your thoughts will be led astray from a sincere and pure devotion to Christ" (II Cor. 11:3).

A sincere devotion to Christ arises only in the context of the Plan of Redemption, rooted in Genesis, even in the report of a tempting serpent. You just can't reject Genesis, or try to explain it away, without cutting strands of revelation woven by the Holy Spirit into the Bible and thus into Christianity.

The Great Divide opens here in a choice like the one faced by Adam and Eve there in the Garden between:

1. The God of Christianity who asks of us the "love" of obedient acceptance of His Word,

OR

2. The gullible arrogance of evolution with its "Did God say...?"

GENESIS

Reveals that human death, spiritual and physical, entered creation as consequence of the Fall.

EVOLUTION

and

THEISTIC EVOLUTION

Theorize that human death is normal inheritance from the animal, thus naturalizing death and thus robbing it of witness to sin and call to repentance.

11

"You Shall Surely Die . . ."
(Gen. 2:17)

Death is not natural to man.

Every gravestone cries out against the triumph of this "last enemy" (I Cor. 15:26).

Man senses that he was not made to die, neither spiritually nor physically.

How, then, did this enemy break into a world made "very good"?

St. Paul sums up what we have already learned: "Therefore as sin came into the world through one man and death through sin, and so death spread to all men because all men sinned. . .even over those whose sins were not like the transgression of Adam, who was the type of him who was to come" (Rom. 5:12, 14).

Death, the unnatural, witnesses to man's sin and Fall. So it is for Christianity.

But it is not so at all for evolution.

Death is as natural to evolutionary man as breathing.

One of the conspicuous sins against Light committed by evolutionary theorists, including theistic evolutionists, is the naturalization of death.

In the evolutionist's world, death does not witness to sin or Fall. Death simply reflects an exhaustion of natural energies. Indeed most evolutionary "evidence" depends on the realm of the dead.

Evolution cannot ask, "Why death?" It takes death, as it takes life, for granted.

Death is at home in the evolutionist's world from the moment that the echoes of the Bang "die" away.

Evolution makes no provision for an original creation in which human death was alien. Theistic evolution has no place for death as penalty on a Fall because it has no perfection to "fall" from and no Fall to confess.

Again, the Great Divide between Christianity and evolution on the understanding of death:

1. Theistic evolution joins secular evolution to blunt what is for Christianity the "sting" of God's sharpest, most frightening and painful reminder of our Fall and its sinful consequence (I Cor. 15:56).

2. Evolution makes death so natural that it loses what is in Christianity its threatening incentive to repentance and redemption. Death is not, for evolution,

as it is for Christianity, the "last enemy" (I Cor. 15:26), but simply the last event.

3. Still more, and worst of all, evolution makes the death of Christ a kind of dramatic gesture, an act detached from any Plan of Salvation. Why, on evolutionary grounds, should God's Son *die* to atone an original sin and guilt which, for evolution, man never incurred? Indeed, what, for evolution, has death to do with sin at all? But, if *death* is not a penalty on sin, then Christ's *dying* cannot pay that penalty. And evolution thus negates the whole Plan of Redemption.

Choice is inescapable:

1. Did death, as Christianity teaches, come into the world because of Adam's sin; **OR** is death, as evolution presumes, only another of the processes natural to man's slow route of development?

2. Is death a stubborn witness to sin, both original and as daily multiplied in our own continuing disobedience, as Christianity holds; **OR** has death, as in evolutionary theory, no witness and admonitory value at all?

3. Is the substitutionary death of Christ on the Cross payment in kind for the death pronounced by God on sin, **OR** can Christ be detached from Genesis and the Old Testament and fitted into theistic evolutionary speculation?

Whatever your personal choice between each set of alternatives, one thing is unmistakable: a Great Divide yawns between Christianity's and both forms of evolution's understanding of death.

Let us ask, in passing, why Jesus wept at the grave of Lazarus (John 11:35).

Was it because, on evolutionary grounds, Lazarus had progressed no further up the ladder of human development? Jesus was saddened, then, by man's lack of evolutionary development? Nothing in the biblical account of this miracle allows that interpretation.

Was it, then, because Jesus could not, if He wished, return Lazarus from the dead?

Not at all. That was exactly what He intended to do.

Was it because Lazarus had no hope of eternal life?

No. Jesus had already assured Lazarus' sister Martha of the resurrection (John 11:24–27).

Why, then, did Jesus weep?

Surely not because Jesus was looking at the grave through the eyes of a theistic evolutionist, but rather because Christ knows most of all that death is absolutely alien to God's design for mankind. Jesus saw in death an indubitable sign of the Fall as recorded in Genesis. He saw in the tomb of Lazarus an ugly witness to the devastation wrought by sin in a creation once "very good," indeed a creation called into existence through Himself.

Jesus sees death as what need not have been . . . and Jesus weeps.

He was there at the Fall, and He stands here at the tomb in anguish over a Fall that corrupted both human history and the universe made for man's subduing, and will soon bring Him, "the Lamb of God," to the Cross in expiation.

There is only a Great Divide between this Christian understanding of the Lord's tears and the evolutionist's bland acceptance of death as natural to human, because natural to animal, history.

Praise God that the believer's assurance that "death shall be no more" (Rev. 21:4) does not rest on the evolutionary ascent of man, nor the patchwork hybrid of theistic evolution. The "death of death" is assured by the Plan of Salvation, because the penalty of death was vicariously paid on Calvary by Him who knew why He wept at the tomb.

Is death, then, as Christianity teaches, not only grim proof of man's Fall but also a relentless call to repentance for the sins that bring death about?

OR

Does death testify only to the exhaustion of man's vital energies, as evolutionists hold?

How Great a Divide this difference makes!

12

GENESIS

Reveals that the essence of sin is willful refusal to heed the Word of God.

EVOLUTION

and

THEISTIC EVOLUTION

Refuse to bow before God's Word in Genesis and elsewhere in the Scriptures.

The Great Divide becomes unmistakable.

12

"Against Thee, Thee Only, Have I Sinned..."
(Ps. 51:4)

King David had sinned in particularly gross fashion.

The poignant fifty-first psalm is his confession.

The story is familiar. David desired Bathsheba, the wife of Uriah, one of his soldiers. David contrives to take Bathsheba and to have Uriah killed. The prophet Nathan is sent by God to confront King David with his guilt (II Sam. 11–12).

David sees himself in the clear light of the prophet's Word, and pens this psalm of abject confession and contrition.

What David did, we know. But why was that "sin"?

Genesis reveals the answer to that question. It sheds

the light of the Word on "sin" in its first and original manifestation.

David did what Adam and Eve had done. He preferred his will to God's. David was guilty of covetousness, of adultery and of murder – all forbidden by God's Word.

The essence of "sin" is ever the same, from the first transgression of Adam and Eve to the end of time: deliberate refusal to "hear," which in the Bible means to do, the Word of God.

David's sin follows the pattern set in Eden, rebellion against God done in yielding to temptation.

Notice what else David says: ". . . and done that which is evil in thy sight" (Ps. 51:4).

David's distinction is instructive.

Sin is done against God's will; sin can bear fruit in *evil* done to one's self and others. Sin is vertical disobedience; evil is horizontal disobedience – both in violation of the divine Law, summarized in the commands to love God above all and our neighbor as ourselves (Matt. 22:37–40).

The evolutionist, like everyone else, is of course acquainted with human evil. We all know something of the inhumanity which men practice on others and on themselves. Who could miss it?

But Christianity teaches that sin is violation of the will of God, as revealed in His Word, with the evil done by man to man as sin's baleful fruit.

If the evolutionist, secular or theistic, really understood the nature of sin, he would find himself condemned first of all.

For, evolutionary theorists do not disprove God's revelation; they simply flout it as did Adam and Eve, which is, as Genesis reveals, *sin!*

Genesis clearly reveals that the essence of sin is the

refusal to "hear," that is, to be governed by, God's Word. And just that Word as revealed through Genesis is the first casualty fallen to evolutionary theorizing. The evolutionist deliberately declines to permit his thinking to be governed by God's Word as revealed through Genesis. He prefers to be ignorant of the Genesis revelation of the nature of sin, lest he find himself judged by it and found wanting.

Faith, we have already pointed out, submits our thoughts, our words and our behavior to control by God's will as revealed through His Word.

"My sheep," Jesus says, "hear my voice..." (John 10:27). His "voice" is the Word proclaimed by Scripture. His "voice" is precisely the Genesis Word which evolution rejects and theistic evolution perverts to its own purposes.

How can the theistic evolutionist claim Him as Lord whose "voice" he will only selectively hear on his own terms?

Having rejected the Word in Genesis, the credulous and the gullible listen to what the Lord calls the voice of "strangers." It is a voice which the believer simply cannot hear: "A stranger they will not follow," Jesus says, "but they will flee from him, for they do not know the voice of strangers" (John 10:5).

Jesus commends instead of gullibility the wisdom of simple faith: "Truly, I say to you, unless you turn and become like children, you will never enter the kingdom of heaven" (Matt. 18:3).

And do you know what children do most of all?

They listen to the Word of their Father! They believe that Word, and give their lives to doing what they hear.

Genesis teaches us to recognize "sin" precisely where

it seems least likely to be found, in very learned and
erudite company, in the salons of fashion, even in the
pulpits disobedient to the Word—wherever the voice of
the Word is silenced by rejection, wherever the light of
the Word is shrouded in the twilight of speculation.

See Adam and Eve standing before the forbidden
tree.

The sun is shining, the sky azure blue, the breeze
caressing, and the scenery that of the world as it left the
Word of God.

Moreover, the man and the woman seemed to behave
as anyone might in the presence of desirable fruit. They
looked; they desired; they took; they ate, perhaps with
impeccable manners. Adam certainly permitted Eve to
nibble first, as only a gentleman should.

How was this almost casual eating "sin"?

What was wrong with this little snack there under
the trees—almost a passing incident in the day?

Bad fruit? No, it appears that it was good fruit, or so
it looked to Eve: "So when the woman saw that the tree
was good for food, and that it was a delight to the
eyes..." (Gen. 3:6).

What was the fault?

Just one little...no, just one gigantic, all-encom-
passing thing: eating of that tree was disobedience to
God's Word. It betrayed the absence of "love," just as
disobedience to that Word always does.

That was all; and that was enough.

Genesis reveals for all time the paradigm, the model,
the type of human "sin."

Adam and Eve banished God's Word from control of
their minds and conduct. They "exchanged the truth for
a lie," as St. Paul will describe it later, "and worshipped
the creature rather than the Creator, who is blessed for
ever! Amen" (Rom. 1:25).

It was a sin no different in kind from all evolutionists' refusal to permit the Word as revealed in Genesis to govern their thinking, who thus willfully exchange the truth for the lie. "And," writes St. Paul, "since they did not see fit to acknowledge God, God gave them up to a base mind and to improper conduct" (Rom. 1:28).

If you stand up for Genesis, you will taste a little of how "base" a mind and what kind of "conduct" evolutionism can produce.

Genesis reveals that the refusal to have God in man's consciousness can appear in settings as lovely as the Garden, as stately as cathedrals, as comfortable as living rooms, as opulent as private clubs, as "learned" as academia, as exclusive as laboratories, as imposing as banks of computers.

And learn that however impressive the surroundings, where Light is denied there darkness rules.

Yes, a repast under Eden's tree reveals the nature of sin.

Its fruits in evil are beyond counting, but its nature is ever the same: sin is barring God's Word from the mind, and thus yielding to the Tempter's, "Did God say?"

The Great Divide rises between:

1. Those who bring their thinking into subjection to God's Word as revealed in all the Scriptures, beginning with Genesis;

OR

2. Those who will not have God in their minds and thus controlling their thoughts, and who reveal their rebellion in their rejection of Genesis either directly or by trying to explain away what it says.

PART THREE

The Plan of Redemption
Incarnation

Resumé

We structure this book, as we have already pointed out, on the Plan of Redemption, rejected by secular evolution and distorted into another religion by theistic evolution and "creationomic science."

Immediately after the Fall, God announces His Plan in the promise made to Eve and the condemnation pronounced on the serpent (see chapter 15).

A new heaven and a new earth will replace a creation corrupted in man's disobedience.

The redeemed in Christ will be ushered into the new creation as the old is destroyed.

Man's guilt and sin are washed away in the blood of Christ, who comes as the "Lamb of God" in fulfillment of the ceremonial system revealed to, and required of, Israel.

The Gospel calls on all for "the obedience of faith"

(Rom. 1:5), and those who respond are schooled by the Spirit in the Word through the Church.

The first step in obedience is self-denial.

The first effect of self-denial is subjecting all thought, desire, and will to the revealed Word of God. Thus, through faith, the believer fits himself into the Plan of Redemption. This is the Christian religion.

The Plan is of one texture from the beginning. Its fundamentals and pattern are established in Genesis.

If Genesis be rejected, outright or by manipulation, Christianity itself is perverted into another religion, one in which man becomes the final authority for what is true, God is used to serve the interests of "science," and Christ is used to guarantee salvation without obedience to His Word, beginning with Genesis.

This is the Great Divide which separates Christianity from evolution, all brands.

In this section we point to aspects of redemption in Christ which are immediately related to strands drawn out of Genesis.

CHRISTIANITY

Teaches that the Word through whom all things were
made becomes flesh, the human flesh prepared for the
Incarnation since the creation of Adam and Eve.

THEISTIC EVOLUTION

Theorizes that Jesus Christ, who has no relation to
the Word through whom all things were spoken into
existence, appears in the flesh man has inherited from
the animal, while secular evolution treats the Incarnation as it does the creation, as myth.

13

"And the Word Became Flesh . . ."
(John 1:14)

Matthew and Luke describe in some detail the birth of Jesus Christ. These accounts underlie the celebration of Christmas.

St. John adds to the Christmas story by very deliberately identifying the babe born in Bethlehem with the Word through whom all things were made: "In the beginning was the Word, and the Word was with God and the Word was God. He was in the beginning with God; all things were made through him, and without him was not anything made that was made" (John 1:1–3).

Theistic evolution pays effusive lip service to God as present in Jesus Christ. But it denies, or circumvents, the Genesis account of God's creation of all things through the Word who became Jesus Christ.

But who, then, is this Jesus of theistic evolution?

He cannot be the Jesus of the Bible.

The Jesus of the Bible is the Word of Genesis: "And God said. . . ."

St. John, though he certainly would be authority enough, is not the only inspired witness who deliberately identifies Jesus the Christ with the Word through whom God created all things: "He is the image of the invisible God, the first-born of all creation; for in him all things were created. . .through him and for him" (Col. 1:15). "But in these last days he has spoken to us by a Son, whom he appointed heir of all things, through whom also he created the world" (Heb. 1:2). Again: "By faith we understand that the world was created by the word of God. . ." (Heb. 11:3).

The Jesus who is the heart of Christianity does not first affect the course of human history after His birth in Bethlehem. The Jesus of Christianity is the Creator-Word first revealed through Genesis. A Jesus cut off by theistic evolution from the Word of Genesis is not the Jesus of Christianity.

That is why we are pointing out that theistic evolution fabricates another religion disguised as Christianity (see also, chapter 16 below).

Epilogue

St. Luke reports that there was no room in men's dwellings for the Babe of Bethlehem. Jesus came to birth in human flesh in a stable.

But God had from "the beginning" uniquely prepared the *human flesh* which received Him (see chapter 6).

The Plan of Redemption did not proceed through a series of fortuitous steps, improvised as the occasion required.

The creating Word freely chose "before the foundation of the world" to become "the Lamb who was slain" (Rev. 13:8). And God the Father prepared through the Word a flesh to incarnate Jesus Christ.

And we repeat that this careful preparation is revealed to the eye of faith in the creation of Eve. She is very deliberately made of the flesh of Adam, so all mankind could be of *one* flesh, the flesh adopted by God's Son.

Genesis is surely written to assure us that Christ did not become just any flesh, nor did He assume a flesh which itself had evolved from the animals.

Jesus became *man* by assuming man's *flesh*.

Jesus became *man* by participation in the "one blood" which God assigned through Adam to all men.

This cannot be, however, the Jesus tacked onto evolutionary theory, who became incarnate in flesh of who knows what antecedents.

This is of utmost concern to you, as is the discrimination of Christianity from evolution at this crucial point.

The flesh which Jesus Christ took on Himself is our flesh, the very same flesh preserved from Adam, through Eve, to ourselves.

There are those who fondly trace their ancestry as far back as records can be found. The record of everyone's ancestry, however, is traced in the Scriptures back to "the beginning." We are all of one flesh and one blood, and can rejoice that it is so. For into this line of human descent from one set of parents, Eve made out of Adam, the Word of creation was joined—joined, then, to you and us and all mankind.

Consider how carefully the line of fleshly descent which we share and which divine royalty assumed on our behalf was prepared:

1. God forms Adam from the dust of the earth, not out of some other flesh (Gen. 2:7).

2. God forms Eve out of one of Adam's ribs, not from some other flesh (Gen. 2:21–22).

3. God the Holy Spirit, in fulfillment of prophecy (Isa. 7:14), miraculously arranges lodging in human flesh for the Son through the Virgin Mary.

4. Mary provides this fleshly "home" for the Son through a decisive act of obedience to the Word of God: "Behold, I am the handmaid of the Lord; let it be to me according to your word" (Luke 1:38). Again, the ever active Word of revelation! Mary's obedience to the Word counterpoises Eve's disobedience to the Word. This leads some theistic evolutionists to rank Mary as Mother of the Church, inasmuch as they have no Eve for Mary to counterbalance. But this is simply another testimony to the distortion which theistic evolution introduces into Christianity.

The credulous may scoff at the Genesis report of the creation of Eve, and the gullible may sneer. What else can unbelief do in the presence of faith? For the believer finds infinite comfort and ground for rejoicing in recognizing his own flesh in the inspired revelation: "And the Word became flesh and dwelt among us, full of grace and truth; we have beheld his glory, glory as of the only begotten Son of the Father" (John 1:14).

The only Son takes the only flesh ever given to man. Your flesh, and ours, and everyone's. So it was planned from the beginning when God took Eve from the side of sleeping Adam.

And Jesus, the Incarnate Word, took our flesh to His

cross and into the grave, raised it up on the third day and rose with it to heaven: "We have this as a sure and stedfast anchor of the soul, a hope that enters into the inner shrine behind the curtain, where Jesus has gone as a forerunner on our behalf..." (Heb. 6:19–20).

For Christianity, the creating Word becomes flesh, the human flesh prepared for Him through the making of Adam and Eve.

For theistic evolution there is no creating Word, but only a process out of which another "Jesus" evolves. If it were otherwise, the principle of uniformity, on which evolutionary theory rests, would be no more.

BECAUSE
GENESIS

Reveals that the essence of sin is self-*assertion*, we can understand why Christ's antidote to sinning is self-*denial*.

BECAUSE
EVOLUTION

and

THEISTIC EVOLUTION

Declare that the key to human progress is the form of self-assertion which results in the "survival of the fittest," the Great Divide between Christianity and evolution becomes still more clear.

14

"Let Him Deny Himself . . ."
(Matt. 16:24)

The Genesis account of the Fall reveals the nature of sin as *self-assertion*, exercised in the refusal to heed God's Word.

Jesus picks up this Genesis thread by demanding *self-denial* of those who would find new life in Him: "Then Jesus told his disciples, 'If any man would come after me, let him deny himself and take up his cross and follow me'" (Matt. 16:24). It is a self-denial exercised in obeying God's Word: "Whoever does the will of God is my brother, and sister, and mother" (Mark 3:35).

Sin is self-assertion. It may appear in very polite, sophisticated, even pious forms. It appears in unctuous garb in theistic evolution, paying excessive lip-service to God's Word while following its own.

Sin's nature is always the same as it was the first time: my will be done!

The Lord requires believers to pray for sin's antidote: "thy will be done...on earth as it is in heaven" (Matt. 6:10).

Jesus illustrates throughout His whole life the obedience to God's Word which led Him ultimately to the Cross (see Epilogue), and in the Garden of Gethsemane set His obedience clearly against Adam's disobedience in the Garden of Eden. Our parents had behaved on this principle: my will be done. In that awful hour in Gethsemane, Jesus, the Second Adam (Rom. 5:14; I Cor. 15:45), prays in the face of impending crucifixion, "...nevertheless not my will, but thine, be done" (Luke 22:42).

The self-assertion of the first Adam dropped man into the abyss and, multiplied in all of Adam's descendents, brings the Second Adam to the Cross in self-denial.

There is no mistaking the relation established in the Plan of Redemption between Eden and Gethsemane. We can hope to understand at least something of the self-denying agony in Gethsemane only in the context of the arrogant self-assertion in Eden.

And we may wonder again how those who deny the Adam of the Garden of Eden can hope to find salvation in the Second Adam who passed through Gethsemane.

And how does all this concern you?

Self-denial begins in letting God's Word, not your (or others') desires or opinions or conclusions, govern your own thoughts.

Take note how the Genesis thread of man's arrogant, "My will be done..." runs out into society to be echoed in phrases like Darwin's "survival of the fittest"—

where the "fittest" as like as not turn out to be the most ruthlessly self-assertive.

Observe how self-assertion against God's Word reveals itself in theories of evolution and in the subtle evasions of theistic evolution.

See how Christ's antidote for sin is drawn out of the Genesis description of what sin is. The self-destroying sin of self-assertion appeared before the forbidden tree of Eden. The redemptive self-denial of obedience is displayed in all its sublime horror on the "tree" of Calvary.

Note how carefully Jesus prescribes the instrument of self-denial: "Take up your cross," the Lord says:

1. The Cross becomes the sign of obedience to the Word of God (see Epilogue).

2. It is on the Cross of Calvary that Jesus, in self-denial unto death, pays the penalty for Adam's self-assertion unto death. All of the pride and arrogance natural to us as fallen must be nailed to our own cross of self-denying obedience to the Word–Genesis not excepted!

3. The symbolism itself derives, you will note, from Genesis by way of Moses' raising of the serpent in the wilderness (see chapter 15). It is on the "tree" of Calvary that the Lord cancels out the sin done by man through the "tree" of Eden.

4. St. Paul sums it all up this way: "I appeal to you, therefore, brethren, by the mercies of God, to present your bodies as a living sacrifice, holy and acceptable to God, which is your spiritual worship. Do not be conformed to this world, but be transformed by the renewal of your mind, that you may prove what is the

will of God, what is good and acceptable and perfect"
(Rom. 12:1–2).

The Great Divide, then, for you:

1. The Genesis thread of self-assertion in the first
Adam, forgiven and cancelled out in the self-denial of
the Second,

OR

2. The self-assertion of the first Adam, reaffirmed in
evolutionary theories and their credo, "the survival of
the fittest."

GENESIS

Anchors the biblical Plan of Redemption epitomized by Jesus Himself in John 3:16:

> For God so loved the world that he gave his only Son, that whoever believes in him should not perish but have eternal life.

Although often quoted as a summary of the heart of Christianity, this text also glows as a diamond in the biblical Plan of Redemption.

EVOLUTION

Dismisses Genesis.

THEISTIC EVOLUTION

Explains away the words of Genesis as not meaning what they say. John 3:16 has to be fitted onto a religion which is so departed from the Plan of Redemption as to be no longer Christian.

15

From Genesis
to Nicodemus

What has one of the favorite texts in the New Testament, John 3:16, to do with Genesis?

Just this: John 3:16 cannot be understood apart from God's revelation through Genesis. The great promise made by this text belongs only to those who believe it in the light of believing Genesis.

Consider, and decide for yourself:

Jesus was speaking early in His ministry, you recall, to the Jewish leader Nicodemus who prudently visited Him at night.

Remember that before He comes to what is reported in the popular sixteenth verse of this third chapter, Jesus has already made reference to an Old Testament event and applied it to Himself. That event was Moses' raising of the bronze serpent in the wilderness, which was, Jesus says, prophetic of His own coming crucifixion.

First, however, the favorite text: "For God so loved the world that he gave his only begotten Son, that whoever believes in him should not perish but have eternal life" (John 3:16).

A favorite text indeed, the more so when we see how it collates themes, or threads, out of Genesis.

Threads out of Genesis appear here?

Yes, without them the text cannot be understood. Notice:

"God so loved the world . . ."

Had God made the world so perfect as to be lovable? Yes, no doubt. He made it all "very good" (Gen. 1:31). But that, as immediately appears, is not Jesus' meaning here.

"That he gave his only begotten Son . . ."

Why should God "give" His Son to demonstrate His love for the world?

Why should "love" for even a perfect world entail such enormous sacrifice?

Now we recall what Jesus had already said to Nicodemus: "And as Moses lifted up the serpent in the wilderness, so must the Son of Man be lifted up, that whoever believes in him may have eternal life" (John 3:14).

Our Lord's reference is to a significant incident in Israel's journey through the wilderness after liberation from Egypt. The people were murmuring against God, as they traveled around the land of Edom. The manna from heaven which, Jesus reveals, foretold His own coming down from heaven (John 6:31–33), displeased the Israelites: ". . . and we loathe this worthless food" (Num. 21:5).

So God loosed among them "fiery serpents," whose sting was mortal.

Then God offers a way out. He instructs Moses to make a bronze serpent and to raise it up on a pole, promising that whoever looked at that substitute serpent would be healed of the poisonous venom absorbed from real serpents. As many as obeyed were cured (Num. 21:4–9).

Obviously, as Christ Himself implied, this event foretold His own vicarious crucifixion. But vicarious, that is substitutionary, for what? and why?

This wilderness encounter was not man's first brush with the serpent. And we are pointed back to another "tree," and to another serpent whose "sting" lay in tempting man into sin and death.

Jesus is drawing a crucial parallel between the raising of the serpent in the wilderness and His own being "raised" on the Cross of Calvary. And we can understand why.

The cure for serpent-sting which God prescribes through Moses obviously points ahead to the Cross on Calvary where the sting of death (I Cor. 15:56) suffered through the serpent in Eden is atoned and overcome. This is why God "gave his only begotten Son." It is His plan to do so because unless God Himself suffers the penalty decreed upon man's sin, there is no hope of redemption. Fallen man has no power to restore communion with God through the expiation of his sins. That depends on Calvary.

It is in the Plan of Redemption that God decides to give His Son to the Cross. God gives because man has forfeited the power to save himself. God loves enough to give even His only Son. And the Son loves enough to undergo on the Cross the penalty of death laid upon the Fall.

We are being taught by Christ Himself in this favorite text to view Calvary in the light of divine revelation in Genesis. Otherwise we do not understand the text at all. He traces His forthcoming crucifixion back through the brass serpent (brass combines two elements as Christ combined God and human flesh!) to the serpent sting in the Garden.

The Genesis-connection becomes even more clear as the Lord goes on:

"That whoever believes in him should not perish . . ."

The Lord defines the Great Divide: believe **OR** perish.

But why that alternative? Why "perish"?

Again, without Genesis who could understand that awesome choice?

In the light of Genesis, we see it all as involved in the Plan of Redemption: man is made perfect; man falls and inherits death; mankind indeed will perish unless God provides His Son as "the lamb of God" through whose sacrificial death on the Cross all who believe may be cleansed of guilt and liberated for redemption.

John 3:16 briefly summarizes the Plan of Redemption.

But the Plan of Redemption has nothing in common

with evolutionary speculation. What place would Moses' raising of the serpent in the wilderness, with its obvious recollection of the serpent in the Garden, have in a theistic evolutionary scheme which denies the Garden? And what place could that event have in God's evolutionary "strategy"? But what biblical meaning could Calvary have without the background of the serpent?

The "Jesus" claimed by the theistic evolutionist cannot be the Jesus who explains His coming by John 3:16.

What the Lord means by "perish" is certainly not some kind of evolutionary lag which His death compensates. Rather, He clearly refers to the penalty of death laid by His Father on all mankind at the Fall, and rehearsed by the sting of the serpents in the wilderness.

Without the raising of Christ on the Cross, prefigured by the serpent raised by Moses, and pointing to the tempting serpent in Eden, mankind was destined to "perish" by virtue of the Fall. That is a destiny which evolution, by its unbelief, simply confirms.

"But have everlasting life."

And what is this "life"?

Life is the restoration of the communion with God lost in the Fall, as discussed in chapters 5 and 11.

This "life" is not given as the crown of some evolutionary process, but to the faith which receives the Word of God as true.

Cut off from the source of life in what happened before the tree in Eden, man can be restored to life, through faith, only by what happened on the "tree" (I Peter 2:24) of Calvary, as symbolized by that "tree" Moses raised in the wilderness.

This is Christianity.

But all the background which gives meaning to John 3:16 is missing in evolution and theistic evolution.

Nicodemus could understand well enough, of course, the strands out of Genesis and Numbers which the Lord was weaving into what has become across the centuries this favorite promise of life eternal. He understood so well that after Christ had been "lifted up" to die on Calvary he joined those who prepared the Lord's body for burial (John 19:39).

Only faith produces learners as ready as he.

Only the credulous and the gullible can hope to attach the Jesus of John 3:16 to evolutionary theories which reject or pervert the Genesis elements of the Plan of Redemption.

THE BIBLE

Reveals that the most Author-itative confirmation of God's revelation through Genesis is made by Jesus Christ.

EVOLUTION

Assumes that such confirmation can be brushed aside or ignored altogether.

THEISTIC EVOLUTION

Also *assumes* that such confirmation can be brushed aside or ignored altogether, while still claiming Jesus as some sort of Reconciler of man with God.

16

Jesus Certifies Genesis

Evolution, by and large, pays no attention to Christianity and the Bible. The Bible is assumed to be but the product of some natural process.

Theistic evolutionists seem to want Jesus without Genesis, or only with a Genesis acceptable to them on their own terms.

But Jesus Himself resists such selective adoption.

The Jesus of the Bible and Christianity goes out of His way to certify the reliability of the Genesis account of creation.

Nor is this surprising when we consider St. John's identification of the Word through whom, according to Genesis, all things were made with Jesus Christ. How could the Lord repudiate Himself?

As Jesus was assembling His cadre of twelve disciples, He found Philip in Galilee and said to him, "Follow me."

Philip hastens to Nathanael with Good News. He says, "We have found him of whom Moses in the law and also the prophets wrote, Jesus of Nazareth, the son of Joseph" (John 1:45).

By the phrase "in the law," Philip points to the *Torah*, Hebrew for "law," meaning the first five books of the Bible. Philip certifies Moses as the author of the "Law," the five books we commonly call the Pentateuch. Jesus is, Philip says, Him of whom Moses wrote. Philip in effect urges Nathanael to come to Jesus by way of Moses, specifically by way of Genesis.

It is a pattern which Jesus Himself employs.

After His resurrection Jesus walks the road to Emmaus with the two disciples who are saddened by His death and mystified by reports of His rising again to life.

Jesus charges them with foolishness for failure to understand the roots of His mission in the Old Testament: "O foolish men, and slow of heart to believe all that the prophets have spoken!"

"Foolish men" is a strong condemnation. Jesus once warned us against using it: ". . . and whoever says, 'You fool!' shall be liable to the hell of fire" (Matt. 5:22).

What the Lord is going to point out is that the Plan of Redemption is clearly revealed through Moses and the prophets, so clearly that only the "foolish" blind themselves to it. For the account goes on: "And beginning with Moses and the prophets, he interpreted to them in all the scriptures the things concerning himself" (Luke 24:27).

We have been talking often in these pages about the

"strands" of revelation rooted in Genesis and woven by the Spirit into the fabric of the Scriptures. The model for so doing is Jesus Himself: ". . . he interpreted in all the scriptures the things concerning himself" — *beginning* with Moses!

The model is unmistakable: the Plan of Salvation begins with the writings of Moses. Only the "foolish" decline to see it.

The Lord permits no leaping over Moses to get to Himself.

The encounter enroute to Emmaus was not the only time that Jesus traced His own role in the Plan of Redemption back to Moses, that is, to Genesis.

In dispute with Jewish unbelief, the Lord is even more emphatic: "If you believed Moses, you would believe me, for he wrote of me. But if you do not believe his writings, how will you believe my words?" (John 5:46–47).

How else can this clear warning be understood except as the Lord's blunt rejection of every effort to claim Him as Savior while ignoring His Word in Genesis, either directly or by subterfuge?

We can only marvel at theistic evolutionists who would casually attach Jesus to their speculations while blind to His revelation through Genesis and deaf to His warning here in St. John.

Could the Lord be more specific: IF you do not believe Moses, HOW will you believe Me?

Either Genesis *and* Jesus, or no Jesus at all!

But how do we know that when Jesus certifies that Moses wrote of Him, He has reference to Genesis?

Let's ask where Moses did write about Jesus. Just

what did the Lord have in mind by requiring belief in Moses' words to believe His words?

Here are some ways in which Moses wrote of the Lord in Genesis:

1. As already pointed out, St. John identifies the Christ with the creating Word of Genesis. John says, "In the beginning was the Word...all things were made through him.... And the Word became flesh and dwelt among us" (John 1:1, 3, 14). "In the beginning" can refer to only one source and that is Genesis. The Word spoken as reported in Genesis is the Word incarnate in Jesus Christ. How much more directly could Moses have been writing about the Christ than when he reports: "And God said..."?

2. Moses' writing of Jesus is confirmed by St. John, then, and again in Hebrews: "God...has spoken to us by a Son...through whom he created the world" (Heb. 1:2). And again: "...for in him all things were created" (Col. 1:15). The New Testament unanimously attributes the "And God said..." to the Word become incarnate in the Christ, who "beginning with Moses..." sets Himself in the center of the Plan of Redemption.

3. St. Paul teaches that the first Adam was "the type of the one who was to come" (Rom. 5:14). And where do we read about the First Adam? In Genesis, of course.

4. What is commonly called the *proto evangelium*, the first promise of the Plan of Redemption to be realized in Jesus, is announced in Genesis. The Lord God is pronouncing His curse on the tempting serpent and includes this: "I will put enmity between you and the woman, and between your seed and her seed; he shall bruise your head, and you shall bruise his heel" (Gen. 3:15). This has long been understood in the Church as the first announcement of the vicarious death of Christ.

And it is written by Moses in Genesis! It is God's guarantee that the Christ, born in the line of the woman,
shall destroy the power of the demonic Adversary
("your head"), but only at the cost of mortal wound to
Himself ("his heel"). Moses could hardly have written
more specifically about Jesus. And how can anyone
hope to appropriate the promise, Genesis denied or
trifled away?

5. In short, because Jesus Christ stands in the center
of the Plan of Redemption, and because that Plan is
anchored in God's revelation through Genesis, Moses
writes of the Christ as he is inspired to write Genesis.

6. And, clearly, the "tree" of Calvary reflects the
"tree" of temptation described in Genesis as we have
pointed out in chapter 15.

Moses does write of Jesus in Genesis. How will anyone who is deaf to Genesis hear Jesus? The question is
His: "If you believed Moses, you would believe me, for
he wrote of me. But if you do not believe his writings,
how will you believe my words?" (John 5:46–47).

How gullible must one be to take "reconciliation"
through Jesus for granted despite repudiating His
Word in Genesis, and shutting out His warning through
St. John?

Ah, you cannot wait to show how out of date we are in
attributing Genesis to Moses?

You have been told that "scholarship" now "proves"
that Moses could not have written Genesis? Nor even
the whole Pentateuch, for that matter?

Well, then, here is the Divide for you, isn't it, your
choice between faith and gullibility:

1. Jesus Himself vouches for the authorship of Moses.

2. Assorted "experts" rule our Lord mistaken.

And you?

Do you walk in the light of faith, or will you stumble along in the shadows cast by those who professionally minister to the credulous and the gullible?

By the way, the thread of Moses' authorship of the Pentateuch runs through your Bible! Take out your concordance and see.

The Great Divide is fully exposed now.

Christ Himself certifies Genesis.

It *is* Christ-ianity **OR** evolution!

PART FOUR

A Summing Up

17

"SCIENCE" in Capital Letters
(And Quotation Marks)

Are you wondering where we little Davids will flee when the Goliath of evolution unsheathes his "SCIENTIFIC" sword?

Well, David did not flee.

And the original Goliath came crashing down.

David simply took God at His Word.

We must understand that the issue between Christianity and evolution is not fought someplace "out there" in the world, where "SCIENCE" so-called clashes with the Scriptures, and trashes the Book.

There is no such someplace "out there." There never has been.

The battle, like all other attacks on the Bible, is fought out in the minds of persons. The struggle is not "out there," but "in here"—also for you and for us.

The decision is made, person by person, in the mind and heart. The imaginary picture of a Goliath-like evolutionary "SCIENCE" triumphant over a fleeing biblical David exists only on television screens, in school textbooks, and the fertile imaginations of theistic evolutionists.

Man has not driven God to the sidelines of His universe. There are only some men who so delude themselves. Man is far from attaining mastery of his own world, or from understanding even himself, let alone dictating how the world and we came into being. Applied science, as we will note, serves mankind well. But for all that, very little is known—for sure—about the world and those who dwell on it. Do you have a cure for the common cold?

Some know more; some know less; but no one knows very much. Most of the world lies shrouded in mystery.

You don't know why that leaf grows just there on the tree in your yard, nor, really, does anyone else—except God. You can kill a fly, but can't revive it; nor can anyone—except God—produce another. We have traced out the "how" of a few things, the "why" of next to none, and are, as Sir Isaac Newton once said, like children playing on the seashore of the great ocean of the unknown.

"Where were you," God interrogates Job, "when I laid the foundations of the earth? Tell me, if you have understanding" (Job 38:4).

Yes, and where was Darwin? Or the theistic evolutionist?

How much better for a society drained of its moral

vitality by evolutionary theorizing if the evolutionist bent the knee with Job, saying: "Therefore I have uttered what I did not understand, things too wonderful for me, which I did not know...therefore I despise myself, and repent in dust and ashes" (Job 42:3, 6).

O, the modern computer does its marvels, indeed, bolstering the far-reaching claims of evolutionary theorists. Running light years out to the very edge of the universe...but don't ask yours to do any of a thousand simple tasks, like enjoying a sunset, cooking breakfast, or understanding a psalm. God's mysteries as far excel man's masteries in our day as they did in Job's.

The "proof" of evolution survives in some men's minds because others recklessly claim to paper over countless gaps in the "record" with imaginative scenarios.

You take your choice and pay the price or reap the reward.

Choose the darkness of evolutionary speculation, and you bind yourself to a world dominated by the God-defying claims of "experts," a gray world yielding obeisance to the "principle of uniformity" so that calculations can be extended by trios of zeroes, and so that someone can confidently call "today the product of yesterday," as if anyone knows what that means. Is your taking a cup of coffee pre-ordained from the Bang?

Or choose the liberating Word, be freed from the grip of yesterday, and be open to all the adventures which communion with the living God has in store.

"SCIENCE" seeks to validate its claims by chaining a world, and all within it, to the past. Christianity buries the past in Christ's tomb, and leaps into the future through His resurrection.

Take note, if you find it helpful, that evolutionary theories are as faddist as designer clothing, "in" one season and "out" the next. This book could be indefinitely extended with quotes from evolutionists completely at odds with each other—and with what they themselves once touted as unquestionable. A book or two included in our Book Note will alert you to the score. Let us put it in the words of Robert Nisbet, late of Columbia University: ". . . the fact is too obvious to be overlooked, or to be swept under the rug, that, between the essential principles of evolution which Darwin gave to the world and the principles of evolution which recent research in several areas has yielded, there is nearly total conflict" (*Prejudices: A Philosophical Dictionary*, p. 79). So it was, in fact, from the day after Darwin published his *Origin of Species* (1859), all the more so after he published his *Descent of Man* (1871).

Evolutionists seem unalterably agreed on only one thing: they are unanimously unwilling to bow before the Author-ity of God's Word in Genesis. For the rest, their theories are in constantly agitated disarray. The noise of their claims only echoes the clash of their differences; their certainty of tone only disguises the insecurity of their footings. Credulity and gullibility may masquerade as more secure than faith, but the anchorage is not the same. Faith is harbored in the certainty of the Word; credulity and gullibility are tossed on the high seas of speculation.

You may understand the arrogance of evolution as a marginal note alongside the script, "Weak point. Shout loud!"

There is certainty open to man, one stance which rises above all controversy and is immune to all critique: "The testimony of the Lord is sure, making wise the simple" (Ps. 19:7).

The issue, in short, is decided—as we pointed out in the beginning—by what is brought to it: faith **OR** credulity/gullibility.

For the supposed contest between Genesis and evolutionary theory always appears in the form of words, God's Word or man's word.

Whoever comes, like David, in faith finds God's Word infallible, and Goliath easily disposed of. There is in fact no "choice" to be made between the Word of Genesis and the chatter of all the hosts aligned with evolution. The decision was made when faith was given the believer. He is simply surprised to discover that anyone could prefer the speculations of theorists to the certainty of God's Word.

True, whoever comes in credulity or gullibility is indeed impressed by the "weight" of the evidence in favor of evolution and against Genesis—and is no doubt surprised that the believer is unmoved. Unbelief even feigns compassion on anyone so benighted as to accept Genesis. Or the evolutionist cannot restrain some guffaw over the believer's "naivete."

The believer will not mind. He knows whose Word sheds light, and whose spreads darkness.

There is a Great Divide fixed between faith, on the one hand, and credulity/gullibility on the other.

You might care to investigate something of the nature of "scientific" theorizing.

As studies listed in our Book Note demonstrate, the so-called "scientific method" may deceive even its practitioners. Presumably "SCIENCE" consists in coming to conclusions based on accumulated observations of fact. But this is, in fact, manifestly impossible. The world buzzes with "facts." Which ones go with which conclusions?

The "scientist" has to begin with some hypothesis, some thesis which he hopes to test and validate or invalidate. His hypothesis "leads" him to "facts" which will support or contradict it. The hypothesis points to the "facts," not the "facts" to the hypothesis. This is common knowledge. And if the "scientist" is strongly disposed to finding support for his hypothesis, oddly enough most of the "facts" he finds will do just that.

If, now, the field is applied science, it will become clear soon enough if the hypothesis produces workable results. But in theoretical "SCIENCE," like evolutionary "SCIENCE," it may be a long time before others will demonstrate from other "facts" that the theory was mistaken. So it has been in evolutionary "SCIENCE" since long before Darwin. The evolutionist finds "proof" for his theories after he has adopted the theory. Darwin candidly admits that. So it is with evolution now. So it is with theistic evolutionists who pick and choose out of the Scriptures whatever seems to support the views they are committed to promote.

There is no unified body of "fact" which has led with unerring aim to what was touted over the last century as "scientific" demonstration of man's animal ancestry. There has been, in fact, only the wildest disarray of hypotheses. These gained their popularity, not from the "evidence," but out of the credulity and gullibility with which they were received.

Imagination coupled with credulity has given speculative "age" to the earth, and time and place and form to fragments of bone and fossil.

Just give a little time to finding out how much real armor Goliath has on. You may come to think him guilty of indecent exposure.

And grow used to the fact that Goliath's fans will not take kindly to having him disrobed. Your belief in the Word revealed through Genesis may stamp you a "child" among the self-acclaimed "wise" of this world, but stand secure on Jesus' Word: "I thank thee, Father, Lord of heaven and earth, that thou hast hidden these things from the wise and understanding and revealed them to babes; yea, Father, for such was thy gracious will" (Matt. 13:25–26)–to youngsters like David, even.

And Paul draws the conclusion: "What then shall we say to all this? If God is for us, who can be against us?" (Rom. 8:31).

Now it is clear why we titled this chapter "SCI-ENCE" in capital letters and quotation marks.

Science (in lower case and without quotation marks) has a long and honorable history of service to mankind.

The term has reference to organized knowledge, veri-fied by experiment, and put to practical application. Applied science reflects the image of God in man. It produces remarkable achievements, and will no doubt push technological adventure beyond our dreams if the last world war be avoided.

Applied science has no quarrel with faith, nor faith with it. It submits its results to those who can use them. Does the car run? Does the dishwasher work? Are the astronauts delivered safely into space? And so on. The scientists work and put their efforts to the test of excellence.

Such science functions in a universe made for it, and fulfills the original mandate given to mankind: "...fill the earth and subdue it; and have dominion" (Gen. 1:28).

But the "SCIENCE" which claims to invalidate Genesis makes no appeal to the tests of usefulness. Such "SCIENCE" is always someone's speculation, selectively marshalling its own "evidence," to masquerade in true science's clothes, trying to enjoy true science's well-earned respect. But it is only an appeal to credulity or gullibility passing itself off as the sure and certain knowledge available only to faith.

"SCIENCE" claims to exercise the author-ity of applied science, thinking you will never notice the deception—and the credulous and the gullible don't. But it always advertises its character by trying to impose on you instead of being of service to you.

"Beware of false prophets," our Lord warns, "who come to you in sheep's clothing but inwardly they are ravening wolves. You will know them by their fruits..." (Matt. 7:15–16).

To paraphrase: beware of "SCIENTISTS" who come to you as scientists. You will know them by their great, pretentious, hollow claims to explaining better than Genesis the origins of man. These "SCIENTISTS" are unaware of how well they fulfill the prophetic indictment of Jeremiah. The prophet condemns those who, "say to a tree, 'You are my father,' and to a stone, 'You gave me birth,'" and he says, "Know and see that it is evil and bitter for you to forsake the Lord your God" (Jer. 2:27, 19).

Only the credulous and the gullible fail to see that this warning is directed to them.

A favorite theistic evolutionist's ploy is to assert that, after all, God reveals Himself in "two books," that of Holy Scripture and "the Book of Nature." *You* may read only the Bible, he hints, but he reads them both. And it soon turns out that what he "reads" in the Book of Nature not only supplements the Bible but also corrects and amends it. God, you will piously be told, could not, after all, contradict Himself.

But notice that the "two books" parallel is false!

Books come to us in words.

We know who supplied the words which constitute the Bible. It was God the Holy Spirit who inspired the writers: "All scripture is inspired by God. . ." writes Paul (II Tim. 3:16); and, "men moved by the Holy Spirit spoke from God," says Peter (II Peter 1:21). The Bible comes to us as the Word of God.

But in whose words does the so-called "Book of Nature" come?

It has no words of its own. So some man must supply them, of course.

So, the Book of Nature really appears in the words of man.

Now, the trick is obvious, and the choice clear.

The Bible is a book in fact. It comes as the Word of God.

Nature is called a "book" to put something over on you. It comes in the words of man. Only the credulous and the gullible are taken in.

It is simply the question of author-ity:

1. The Bible speaks with the Author-ity of God, appealing to faith.

2. The "Book of Nature" speaks with the author-ity of man, appealing to credulity or gullibility.

Don't be taken in!

But, after all, have we no responsibility toward all that stuff accumulated as "evidence" for evolution? All the stones, bones, caves, layers, skeletons . . . all the squabble about the flood, lost continents, the Galapagos Islands, mastodons and so on . . . ?

Well, as you wish.

If your inclination is to pick and shovel, to reconstruct skeletons, to pursuit of calculations, to imagine lost worlds . . . who is to say?

But the Bible has its priorities. Credulity and gullibility are no substitutes for faith. The Word is preeminent. Obedience to it, starting with Genesis, is obligatory! Your cross may be the obligation to forego speculation, to risk loss of status, even to bear the jeers of the "learned."

And, whatever your calling, there's work to do.

When our Lord delivered to His disciples what is called the Great Commission, as recorded by St. Matthew, He left this instruction for His Church: "Go therefore and make disciples of all nations . . . teaching them to do all I have commanded you" (Matt. 28:19–20).

Teaching "them . . ." means you and us, and all who believe. "To do all . . ." must mean all that is revealed in His Word.

Deal, then, with the fossils, bones, layers and mastodons in the light of all that He asks us to do, beginning with obedience to the Scriptures, which, you recall, He says "cannot be broken" (John 10:35).

The temples of evolutionary worship will one day, like all the temples of unbelief before them, come crashing down.

Consider the Word as revealed through the psalmist:

Our God is in the heavens; he does what he pleases.
[Pause to interject: so much for the principle of uniformity.]
Their idols are silver and gold, the work of men's
hands.
They have mouths, but do not speak; eyes, but do
not see.
They have ears, but do not hear; noses, but do not
smell.
They have hands, but do not feel; feet, but do not
walk; and they
    do not make a sound in their throat.
Those who make them are like them; so are all who
trust in them.
    (Ps. 115:3–8)

An apt enough description of the idol of evolution.
And admonition enough – for faith.
What then?
The Psalmist's command: "O Israel, trust in the
Lord!" (Ps. 115:9).
And St. Paul: "Neither occupy yourselves with myths
and endless genealogies, which promote speculations
rather than the divine training that is in faith"
(I Tim. 4).
Strange as it is may seem, the only key to absolute
certainty in life is faith.
Because faith alone gives access to the infallible
Word of God.
That is why the real aim of all evolutionary specula-
tion is discrediting faith, or the faith-ful.
Why should you be misled?

Epilogue
The Cross

The Plan of Salvation is known by its own, unique sign.

It is the sign of the Cross.

The Cross is easily assumed to be the sign of salvation. As such it is claimed by theistic evolution. Jesus is tacked onto theistic evolution along the way as God is tacked onto it from the beginning.

But the Bible offers no support for such manipulation.

The Cross of Christ is not at our service.

The Cross of Christ is the sign of absolute obedience.

The Cross of Christ is the sign of a very specific kind of absolute obedience, namely *unqualified obedience to the word of God!*

166

Jesus' whole life is governed by, "It is written . . ." in the Scriptures. And the Scriptures begin with Genesis.

"And being found in human form he humbled himself," St. Paul writes, "and became obedient unto death; even death on the cross" (Phil. 2:8).

The Christ makes the Cross the sign of obedience, unqualified and absolute obedience.

The Lord's obedience had a very specific form. He lived and died in total obedience to the Word of His Father, to the Old Testament Word, beginning with Genesis.

This Scripture, He says, ". . . cannot be broken" (John 10:35). And, unlike the evolutionist, Jesus will not break this Word: "Not an iota, not a dot, will pass from the law until all is accomplished" (Matt. 5:18).

Always, Jesus lives in obedience to the Scriptures.

On the night of the Last Supper, He says, "The Son of Man goes as it is written of him . . ." (Matt. 26:24). Later, in the dark confrontation with Judas and the mob, the Lord commands Peter to put away his sword. "Do you not think that I cannot appeal to my Father," He says, "and he will at once send me more than twelve legions of angels?"

Why, then, does He not do so?

Hear the Lord's own Word, spoken out of the agony of obedience: "But how then should the scriptures be fulfilled, that it must be so?" (Matt. 26:53-54). That is, then the Plan of Redemption would have been aborted, and the Scriptures from Genesis to Malachi broken.

It is a question to be faced: will He, who obeys the Scriptures even unto death, give the sign of His Cross, the very weapon of death, to theistic evolutionists who go casually "break" the Scriptures He so scrupulously honored?

The Cross itself arises out of a totally sacrificial life, lived as a series of variations on one theme: ". . . as it is written" – in the Scriptures!

"Christ died for our sins," St. Paul writes, "according to the scriptures. . ." (I Cor. 15:3).

He echoes what Jesus Himself says to His disciples on the day of His ascension: "These are my words which I spoke to you; that everything written about me in the law of Moses and the prophets must be fulfilled" (Luke 24:44).

Obedience was not optional for Him. "Was it not necessary," he asks the puzzled disciples enroute to Emmaus, "that the Christ should suffer these things and enter into his glory?" (Luke 24:26).

If obedience to the Scriptures was "necessary" for the Christ, can it be less for those who would lay claim to His Cross?

No, obedience to the Scriptures is not optional for all who would take on themselves the sign of His Cross: "Whoever does not bear his own cross and come after me, cannot be my disciple" (Luke 14:27).

That is, whoever declines to assume a total obedience to the Scriptures must not imagine that I count him My disciple.

This is the purpose, St. Paul writes to the Romans, for Paul's missionary efforts: ". . . to bring about the obedience of faith for the sake of his name among all nations. . ." (Rom. 1:16).

It was the Lord's own Word, which he heard on the

Damascus road, Paul says to Festus and Agrippa, that he would be sent to the Gentiles, "to open their eyes, that they may turn from darkness to light and from the power of Satan to God, that they may receive forgiveness of sins and a place among those who are sanctified by faith in me" (Acts 26:18).

But what, then, of those who decline to "see" in the Light as revealed through this very Word of God in Genesis?

Consider very thoughtfully, then, for the issue is momentous:

1. The Cross is the sign of obedience to the Scriptures which cannot be broken. These infallible Scriptures begin with Genesis.

2. Can those who think to break the Scriptures by merging Word and evolution into the hybrid of theistic evolution hope to bear the Cross with integrity and find in it the promise of the Plan of Redemption they seek to abort to their own use?

3. "Not every one," Jesus warns us, "who says to me, 'Lord, Lord,' shall enter the kingdom of heaven, but he who does the will of my Father who is in heaven" (Matt. 7:21). Is an effort to unite the revealed will of the Father with the evolutionary speculations of man doing "the will of the Father"?

"Then they said to him, 'What must we do, to be doing the works of God?' Jesus answered them, 'This is the work of God, that you believe in him whom he has sent'" (John 6:28–29).

And who is this Word whom God has sent?

He is the Word through whom all things were made,

as reported in Genesis and confirmed by the New Testament.

He is the substance of the Plan of Redemption as it stretches from "the beginning" in creation and Fall, to the end in re-creation and life eternal.

He is the Word who freely sustains all things in being, who stills the sea and walks beside the faithful.

He is the guarantee of unbounded freedom, who shatters the grip of yesterday on today, and opens wide the dawn of new hope, unlimited option, unending horizon.

And in all this, He is the antithesis of what theistic evolution stands for. His is the power and the laughter that disperses the mists of speculation in the sparkling light of the Word.

It is He who says: "Every one then who hears these words of mine and does them will be like a wise man who built his house upon the rock; and the rain fell, and the floods came, and the winds blew and beat upon that house, but it did not fall, because it had been founded upon the rock" (Matt. 7:21, 24–25).

It is He whose Word will be our Judge at the end: "He who rejects me and does not receive my sayings has a judge; the word that I have spoken will be his judge on the last day" (John 12:48).

And one of the Words which He speaks is this: "If you do not believe his [Moses'] writings, how will you believe my words?" (John 5:47).

It is He, not we, who sets the Great Divide between Christianity and evolution.

"Be not deceived; God is not mocked . . ." (Gal. 6:7).

THE PLAN
OF REDEMPTION
Final Accounting

W e began with pointing out that all religions seek the reconciliation of man to God. What is unique about Christianity is that God provides the Plan of Redemption, and reveals it, beginning with Genesis. In all other religions man maps out his own route to God.

The chart below lists some of the Genesis elements of the Plan of Redemption, and measures them against both evolution and theistic evolution. It will become vividly clear that theistic evolution (including "creationomic science") distorts Christianity into just another man-made religion, as does secular evolution.

The Plan of Redemption

	Genesis	Evolution	Theistic Evolution
1	"In the beginning, God" the Father Almighty	In the beginning, Bang.	In the beginning, Bang plus God, who is used to set off the Bang and to sustain what follows, but is forbidden to interfere with evolutionary processes.
2	"And God said" – God creates through His Son, called the Word.	Denies creation by the Word.	Denies creation by the Word.
3	"And God said, 'Let there be light.'"	Denies the possibility of light without a physical vehicle.	Denies the possibility of light without a physical vehicle.
4	Man is made an adult, in God's image.	Denies making of man as an adult, and has no conception of a divine image.	Denies making of man as adult, and has no way of violating the "principle of uniformity" to fit a divine image on the evolutionary process.
5	God breathes into adult man's nostrils to make him "a living soul."	Ignores.	Would like to believe that somewhere in the evolutionary process God made some animal "human," but cannot accept such intrusion on the order of nature.
6	God makes Eve out of Adam's rib, thus ensuring an integrity of human flesh and blood for Jesus' incarnation.	Denies.	Denies.
7	God sanctifies human marriage in words confirmed by Jesus, and as a model of the relation between Christ and the Church, by having made Eve of Adam's flesh.	Denies, and erodes marriage and the family.	Provides no foundation in creation for the sanctity of marriage, nor for its being a model for the relation of Christ and the Church.

8	God made all things, man included, "very good," thus making man responsible for his own misbehavior.	Has no provision for man's ever being "very good."	Has no provision for man's ever being "very good."
9	God separates His acts of creation into discrete and separate segments.	Development moves without interruption from species to species.	Development moves without interruption from species to species.
10	Man falls from his created perfection through an act of disobedience, and thus plunges all mankind into guilt and depravity.	No provision for a Fall, because no provision for a created perfection to fall from.	No provision for a Fall, because no provision for a created perfection to fall from.
11	Death enters history as consequence of man's Fall, and is an urgent call to repentance.	Naturalizes death.	Naturalizes death.
12	Sin is revealed to be a deliberate violation of God's commands.	No provision for "sin."	Involves God in man's "sin" because man's evolution is God's "strategy" of development.
13	The Word enters the human flesh prepared for Him since the creation, to live and die as "the Lamb of God" whose death "taketh" away the sins of the world.	Even if Jesus be accepted as a good man, has no Plan of Redemption to give meaning to His crucifixion.	Christ dies, not to atone for sin, but to reconcile God to man at the stage man has reached under God's control of the evolutionary "strategy." Christ supplements His Father's "strategic" shortfall.
14	The Plan of Redemption forms the vital structure of Christianity.	Has no Plan of Redemption, hence no claim on Christianity.	Aborts the Plan of Redemption, and perverts Christianity into just another man-made religion.

As the chart demonstrates, theistic evolution concurs far more with secular evolution than with Christianity's Plan of Redemption. The hybrid theory which theistic evolution forges in futile, and often deceptive, effort to bridge the Great Divide is only another of the countless religions of man.

We decline, for reasons spread across the text, to concede that Christianity must, like Elijah, arise and flee the threatening legions of evolutionary speculation. God is not in the wind, earthquake, and fire of arrogant secularism, and above the tumult faith still hears the "still small voice." We salute the "seven thousand who have not bowed the knee" to this Baal of the twentieth century (I Kings 19:9–18).

Book Note

Wₑ do not call this our bibliography. It makes no pretense of being exhaustive. Books on creation, evolution, theistic evolution, and science abound. We mention some that have been useful to us.

Our basic Author-ity: the Bible.

On the Plan of Redemption: the great Confessions, like the Augsburg, the Belgic, and Westminster (and Catechisms); the Heidelberg Catechism. Aulen, G., *Christus Victor*, 1953 (1951).

On evolution: Darwin, C., *Origin of Species*, 1859; *Descent of Man*, 1871. Gish, D., *Evolution: The Challenge of the Fossil Record*, 1985 (critical). Himmelfarb, G., *Darwin and the Darwinian Revolution*, 1968 (1959). Hotton, N., *The Evidence of Evolution*, 1968. Jansma, S., *Six Days*, 1985 (critical). Pittman, M., *Adam and*

Evolution, 1984 (critical). Simpson, G., *The Meaning of Evolution*, 1967.

On theistic evolution: de Fraine, J., *Adam and the Family of Man*, 1965. Dowey, E., Jr., *A Commentary on the Confession of 1967*, 1968. Gunnweg, A., *Understanding the Old Testament*, 1978. *A New Catechism*, trans. out of the Dutch of Jesuit authorship. Process Theology, as represented by J. Cobb, Jr., *God and the World*, 1969. Van Til, H., *The Fourth Day*, 1986 (he prefers "creationomic science"). White, A., *A History of the Warfare of Science with Theology in Christendom*, 1896. Wright, G., *The Old Testament and Theology*, 1969.

On science: Feuer, L., *Einstein and the Generations of Science*, 1974. Koestler, A., *The Act of Creation*, 1964. Wightman, W. *The Growth of Scientific Ideas*, 1953.